SOCCER

Titles in The History of Sports Series include:

SOCCER

BY GAIL B. STEWART

Lucent Books, Inc.
San Diego, California

Library of Congress Cataloging-in-Publication Data

Stewart, Gail, 1949–
    Soccer / by Gail B. Stewart.
        p.   cm. — (History of sports)
    Includes bibliographical references and index.
    Summary: Discusses the origins and evolution of the game of
soccer, as well as memorable events and key personalities
in the game's history.
    ISBN 1-56006-712-8 (hardcover: alk. paper)
    1. Soccer—History—Juvenile literature. 2. Soccer—Social
aspects—Juvenile literature. [1. Soccer—History.] I. Title. II. Series.
    GV943.25 .S82   2001
    796.334—dc21   00-008695

Contents

FOREWORD

More than many areas of human endeavor, sports give us the opportunity to see the possibilities in our physical selves. As participants, we all too quickly find limits in how fast we can run, how high we can jump, how far and straight we can hit a golf ball. But as spectators we can surpass those limits as we view the accomplishments of others and see how fast, how smooth, and how strong a human being can be. We marvel at the gravity-defying leaps of a Michael Jordan as he strains towards a basketball hoop or at the dribbling of a Mia Hamm as she eludes defenders on the soccer field. We shake our heads in disbelief at the talents of a young Tiger Woods hitting an approach shot to the green or the speed of a Carl Lewis as he appears to glide around an Olympic track.

These are what the sports media call "the oohs and ahhs" of sports—the stuff of highlight reels and *Sports Illustrated* covers. But to understand a sport only in the context of its most artistic modern athletes is shortsighted, for it does little justice to the accomplishments of the athlete *or* to the sport itself. Far more wise is to view a sport as a continuum—a constantly moving, evolving process. On this continuum are not only the superstars of today, but the people who first played the sport, who thought about rules and strategies that would make it more challenging to play as well as a delight to watch.

Lucent Books' series, *The History of Sports,* provides such a continuum. Each book explores the development of a sport, from its basic roots onwards, and tries to answer questions that a reader might wonder about. Who were its first players and what sorts of rules did the sport have then? What kinds of equipment were used in the beginning and what changes have taken place over the years?

Each title in *The History of Sports* also identifies key individuals in the sport's history—people whose leadership or skills have made a difference in the way the sport is played today. Included will be the easily recognized names, the Mia Hamms and the Sammy Sosas, the Wilt Chamberlains and the Wilma Rudolphs. But there are also the names of past greats, people like baseball's King Kelly, soccer's Sir Stanley Matthews, and basketball's Hank Luisetti—who may be less familiar today, but were as synonymous with their sports at one time as the "oohs and ahhs" players of today.

Finally, the series looks at the aspects of a sport that are particularly important in its current point on the continuum. Baseball today is better understood knowing about salary caps and union negotiators. One cannot truly know modern soccer without knowing about the specter of fan violence at matches. And learning about the role of instant replay is critical to a thorough understanding of today's professional football games. In viewing a sport as a continuum, the strides that have been made along the way are that much more admirable. It is a richer view, and one that shows how yesterday's limits have been surpassed—and how the limits of today are the possibilities of athletes in the future.

"The Beautiful Game"

THE SCENE AT the Rose Bowl in Pasadena, California, was pandemonium on July 10, 1999. That afternoon a stadium filled with screaming fans—many with face paint and waving large American flags—watched as the U.S. women's World Cup team played China's team for the championship.

The crowd, which included President Bill Clinton and his family, was over 90,000. Another 40 million were watching the game on their televisions. And they saw an exciting game; in the overtime shootout, U.S. defender Brandi Chastain kicked a left-footed shot into the net to give the United States its first-ever World Cup championship.

"The Rose Bowl was so loud we couldn't hear one another," laughs one New Jersey woman who brought her three daughters to the game. "I've never been in a place where the cheering was so loud—it was breathtaking. My kids and I won't ever forget it."[1]

"Not Here, Not in America"

The Rose Bowl's noisy, exuberant crowd was of little interest to European fans, for whom filled soccer stadiums are commonplace.

"We're used to it, that's right," says sixty-two-year-old Gerry Dolan, an Irishman from Belfast who watched the World Cup game on television. "Back in Ireland we love to cheer; it's expected. My friends and I follow the lads to wherever they're playing. We don't so much care about whether they play brilliant or not, but we sing the songs and wear our gear, and the day goes by in a hurry!" he laughs. "It's hard to think of anything else all us old men would travel so far to do."[2]

However, Dolan admits, the experience must have been quite new for Americans. "It's the first time mainstream America has truly embraced soccer, I think," says Dolan. "You see sports-mad fans watching American football, or basketball, but not soccer—not here, not in America. But this time, it seemed like Americans were really into it. It's great for the fans, great for the game as a whole."[3]

Brandi Chastain exults after scoring the winning goal on a penalty kick in the 1999 World Cup final.

A Long Time Coming

The game has had no shortage of fans throughout the rest of the world. Soccer is without a doubt "the world's game," played by more nations than any other sport. In more than 170 countries, national soccer teams vie for the privilege of competing in the World Cup, held every four years.

But on smaller levels, the game is even more embedded in the prevailing culture. No other game is more widely played by children and adults; no other game is more heavily attended by fans. During soccer games in many nations, schools and offices close, factories grind to a halt, and official celebration days are called, providing the favorite team wins. The game's appeal is not restricted to certain racial or economic groups.

One Illinois high school soccer coach says he isn't able to put his finger on the exact appeal of the game, but he knows that it is a powerful one:

> You know, the greatest soccer player that ever lived, Pelé, has called soccer "the beautiful game." Anyone who's watched great soccer knows he's right. It's so amazingly beautiful, it's like no other sport—watching someone like Pelé can take your breath away. And yes, Americans are the poorer for discovering that beauty so late, but it's better than never seeing it at all.[4]

"THE NUMBER ONE PRIORITY"

The American public's very recent interest in soccer is ironic, say enthusiasts, considering how many Americans play the sport. In the United States more young people play soccer than they do baseball, football, or basketball. The American Council on Sports estimated in May 1999 that more than 18 million Americans—almost 5 million of whom were adults—played soccer at least once during the previous twelve months. More than 40 percent of all children between ages six and twelve play regularly in a recreation or club league.

Such statistics are not lost on the multi-billion-dollar sporting goods industry, which sees the sale of soccer shoes, balls, and clothing going through the roof. In an interview with Melissa Levy in the *Knight-Ridder/Tribune Business News*, Nike spokesman Jim Sorrell says that while basketball shoes has been the company's focus during the last decade, Nike sees soccer as its future. "Soccer is the number one priority for this company right now," says Sorrell.

Young Americans are drawn to soccer despite its slow acceptance among adults.

What is the basis of "the beautiful game?" Is its essence in the rules or in the skill of the players? How has the game taken spectators' breath away in virtually every corner of the world?

CHAPTER 1

From Hazy Beginnings

THE WORLD CUP—the most prestigious prize in all of soccer—started in 1930. However, the rules of soccer, as it is played today, were set down in 1863 in London. But soccer—in some form or another—has been played for centuries, in many parts of the world. As much as various countries would like to claim credit for inventing the game, its source is unknown.

Ancient Roots

Five thousand years ago Chinese athletes "juggled" a ball the size of a softball with their feet, thighs, and forehead, keeping the ball aloft as long as possible. It wasn't long, say sports historians, until they organized competitions using such skills.

In 2500 B.C., during the Han dynasty, the game was known as *tsu-chu*—from two words meaning "kicking" and "leather ball." The game was played by two teams; the object was to kick a leather ball filled with female human hair—the significance of which is now unknown—into a net stretched across poles thirty feet high. Players could not touch the ball with their hands.

Tsu-chu continued from dynasty to dynasty, gaining in popularity. Some emperors, feeling that the game increased one's footwork and agility, urged soldiers to play it as part of their daily training and drills. *Tsu-chu* appears in military textbooks from two thousand years ago.

On the other side of the planet, the Aztecs were playing a similar game, but

Although the source of modern soccer is unknown, its roots can be traced to ancient China.

with more violent overtones. They used the game as a means of ensuring a good growing season after planting, using the ball—sometimes the skull of a sacrificed animal—to symbolize the sun.

The movement of the "sun" traveling over the dark field would bring good luck to the Aztecs, and the winners of the game were honored by being sacrificed themselves. "Before cutting off their heads," writes one soccer historian, "[the Aztecs] painted red stripes on their bodies. The cho-

sen of the gods would offer their blood, so the earth would be fertile and the heavens generous."[5]

Harpastum

The ancient Greeks developed a kicking game that, for the first time, was played on a field marked with boundary lines. The ball could be kicked or thrown, and speed and accurate passing were highly praised skills. The game was so much a part of Greek culture, in fact, that the ancient playwright Antiphanes used phrases like "long ball" and "short pass" in his comedies.

The ancient Romans took over the game, naming it *harpastum*. The tackling and hitting permitted in the Roman version of the game was very popular with Roman soldiers. Like the emperors of ancient China, Roman generals realized the game's potential as a conditioning tool for their men, and they urged soldiers to play *harpastum* at least once a day, no matter where they were stationed. Because the Roman Empire engulfed so much of Europe, it is easy to see how the game spread. Within a few years a form of *harpastum* appeared in many parts of Europe. One of the places occupied by the Romans for almost four centuries, beginning in the year A.D. 43, was Britain, or present-day England. The people of Britain were especially fond of the rough and tumble game. Interestingly, it was there, in Britain, that would be the site of most major developments of the game for the next fifteen hundred years.

Anything Goes!

Harpastum, the game that the people of Britain learned from the Roman soldiers, was fairly simple in concept. There were two teams (no rules about how many on a team) and a ball was thrown between them. Whichever team was able to move the ball through the other team and past the opposite end line was declared the winner.

Although the object of the game was simple, in reality *harpastum,* as played in Britain became anything but simple. It was basically a mob game in which "no rules" was the rule. Players could do almost anything to prevent an opposing player from scoring or advancing the ball—kick, hit, punch, slap, and even bite. Evidently such roughness was favored by the Brits, who won the first recorded game against the Romans in A.D. 217 in the town of Derby.

The game continued to be popular long after the Romans left Britain in 409. Its mob character continued, too; the most spectacular games pitted the men of one village against those of a neighboring village. The boundaries of the playing area were sometimes several miles in each direction. The game would continue until the ball—usually an animal bladder filled with air—had been kicked into the opposing team's village.

Historians say that the competition was so fierce that the kicking game frequently degenerated into fistfights. After a game, the ground between villages was littered with the bloody, moaning bodies of players. It was not uncommon for a particularly hard-fought match to result in a death or two.

"A Game of Ball"

By the 1100s, the game was being played in the towns and cities as well as the rural areas. In 1175 a monk named William Fitzstephen described the scene outside his window—a group of young men playing what he described in Latin as *ludus pilae*—"a game of ball." The game Fitzstephen witnessed was being played on a flat patch of ground just outside the city of London. However, as towns became more and more crowded, ball players began using the city streets for their games.

The results were predictably frightening for the townspeople, many of whom barricaded themselves indoors while the loud, rough game thundered past their homes. Rain and snow did nothing to slow the game; quite the contrary—the poor conditions seemed to make the game even more alluring to young players.

Edward III denounced the game of soccer, believing that his soldiers wasted too much time playing it.

It was only a matter of time until the shopkeepers and other citizens complained loudly enough to be heard by the king. In April 1314 King Edward II issued a royal proclamation, noting that such games were a definite menace to public safety: "For as much as there is great noise in the city caused by hustling over large balls . . . from which many evils might arise, which God forbid, we command and forbid on behalf of the King, on pain of imprisonment, such game to be used in the city in the future."[6]

Twenty-five years later, Edward III raised his own objections about the game.

Not only was he irritated by the way people had ignored his father's earlier proclamation, but he was also concerned about the way his soldiers were using their free time. Since the days of ancient Greece and Rome, the rules of war had changed—and with those changes came different expectations for soldiers.

Whereas agility and endurance were critical attributes for soldiers in ancient times, by Edward III's day soldiers were first and foremost marksmen. Instead of marching long distances, soldiers remained in castle towers with bows and arrows ready to defend their domain.

And what good did it do for marksmen to be playing games, Edward III wondered. In 1349 he publicly complained about his fighting men playing "skittles, quoits, fives, football, or other foolish games which are no use."[7] Although the reference was far from positive, it is the first time the game had taken on the name football—the one still used in England today.

Condemnation Doesn't Work

Few players of football were shamed into giving up the game; indeed, it seemed as though the more the monarchy of England condemned it, the more popular it became. Edicts were signed against the game by Henry IV in 1410, by Henry VI in 1447, James III in 1491, and Elizabeth I in 1561—with little result.

NATIVE AMERICAN SOCCER

In their book *America's Soccer Heritage*, historians Sam Foulds and Paul Harris discuss a game played by Native Americans at the time the Pilgrims arrived in 1620. Called *"pasuckquakkohowog,"* meaning "they gather to play football," the game sounded a great deal like early forms of soccer played in England.

More often than not the venue for a game was on a broad sandy beach at Lynn, Revere, or Cape Cod, where playing surfaces approximately a mile long and a half mile wide on hard sand were available at low tide. . . . The goals were sometimes a mile apart and the football was about the size of a handball. It had a cover of deerskin, stuffed with deer hair. . . .

Although thirty to forty men on a side was often the full complement of player strength, at times as many as 1,000 people might participate in the activity. Instead of donning a uniform, the Indians covered themselves with paint and ornaments as if planning to do battle. In this way no one, opponent or teammate, could be identified. It was not uncommon for legs or other bones to be broken during the course of a game and the disguises made it possible for the one who was responsible for the accident to escape detection. In this way retaliation was unlikely.

Despite the attempts of monarchs, the game called football was showing up more and more in the popular culture of the time. In *The Comedy of Errors,* written in 1592, Shakespeare used the game as a means of formulating the complaint of one of his characters:

Am I so round with you as you with me,
that like a football you do spurn me thus?
You spurn me hence, and he will spurn
    me hither,
If I last in this service you must case me
    in leather.[8]

Soccer in the fifteenth and sixteenth centuries was played very much like the game of rugby is today. Players would bunch together and do lots of pushing, elbowing, and kicking. However, it was not as much of a free-for-all as in centuries past; rules against blatant tripping and hitting below the waist had become widespread, although enforcement of such rules was difficult.

The ball looked more like modern soccer balls: an inflated animal bladder that was encased in stitched leather. It was usually brown. The goal had no net, as it does today. Instead, it was two tall sticks set approximately eight to ten feet apart.

"Nothing but Beastly Fury"

The roughness of the sport must have been quite pronounced, for a variety of people took notice of it—not only kings and queens. Sir Thomas Elyot, a diplomat in London during the sixteenth century felt that players were easily risking their lives by playing: "Football, wherein is nothing but beastly fury, and extreme violence, whereof procedeth hurt, and consequently rancour and malice do remain with them that be wounded, whereof it is to be put in perpetual silence."[9]

Another critic of the game, Puritan writer Phillip Stubbs, wrote in painstaking detail about the violence that seemed to him inherent in soccer. He urged that young men think twice before entering into a game since even the winners were in danger:

So that by this meanes, sometimes their necks are broken, sometimes their backs, sometimes their legs, sometimes their armse, sometimes one part thrust out of joynt, sometimes their eyes start out; and sometimes hurt in one place, sometimes in another. But whosoever scapeth away the best goeth not scotfree, but is either sore wounded, [crushed], and bruseed, so as he dyeth of it or else scapeth very hardly.[10]

Seeing the Possibilities

Regardless of the bad publicity that it received, there were some who felt that the game had some possibilities. For example, Richard Mulcaster, a teacher at a boys' school in the late 1500s, thought violence was not a necessary part of the game; he believed that if a few rules could be added, football could be a positive experience for players instead of a risk of life and limb.

He urged that there be fewer players on the field, and he suggested a referee of sorts—someone who would control the fouls on the field. With these two improvements, Mulcaster wrote, there would be

The style of play in the fifteenth and sixteenth centuries resembled the modern game of rugby.

less of "the thronging of a rude multitude, with bursting of shinnes and breaking of legges."[11]

Mulcaster's suggestions may have been partially responsible for the game's development, but it is impossible to be certain to what extent. It is known, however, that the games that once were played by one hundred or more players at once became smaller and a bit more manageable.

Two Kinds of Football

By the nineteenth century the game had become the most popular of all pastimes. In schools, it was a way for boys to "let off a little steam" during the day, and their teachers and priests often played with them.

But the game was actually two games. There were different ways of playing, depending on what school one attended or what part of England one was from. One type of football was known as the handling game. This style was quite rough; players of the handling game would do almost anything to gain and retain possession of the ball. Pushing, kicking, tackling, and elbowing (the biting and punching were forbidden now) were part of the game. Among others, Rugby School was a proponent of this style of football. Eventually, its brand of football

In the handling game of the nineteenth century pushing, kicking, and tackling were common.

The Harrow team of 1867. The school played the dribbling game, a style of football that emphasized teamwork.

would become a separate sport, named for the school.

The other style of football was known as the dribbling game, since dribbling the ball with the feet was an important skill. This game had rules against touching the ball with one's hands and against tripping or grabbing other players, and it emphasized teamwork and speed. There were several prestigious schools that preferred their football this way, among them Eton, Harrow, and Winchester. This style would eventu-

ally become known by the term *football* in England and *soccer* in the United States.

"The Simplest Game"

In the meantime, however, there was a problem among the English schools. Wanting very much to play one another, they were uncertain how to proceed. What rules should they use? Was it permissible to tackle the player with the ball? Could one catch the ball with his hands, or was that a foul?

The answer to all this confusion seemed obvious: Come up with one set of rules on which everyone could agree. But while formulating a set of rules that would please everyone was a good idea, it proved to be impossible.

In 1862 a schoolmaster named J. C. Thring established a set of rules for soccer, which he called "the simplest game." But two of Thring's ten rules were controversial. The second rule forbade players from catching the ball with their hands, and the third warned that kicks had to be aimed at the ball, not at other players.

Devotees of the handling game were furious. Not only did they feel that throwing the ball was a part of the game, but they also thought that hacking (kicking at an opponent's legs and shins) should be fair. The competition between the two groups came to a boil on December 8, 1863, at Freemasons' Tavern on Great Queen Street in London.

The Beginning of Soccer

At this meeting were representatives from various boys' schools and colleges as well as members of men's sporting clubs who also enjoyed playing football. It was hoped that the meeting would result in the formation of a football association whose job it would be to regulate football games throughout England.

But it was apparent to all who attended the meeting that the differences of opinion over the game of football were too wide to be compromised. The greatest argument came over the practice of hacking; when the newly created Football Association (FA) officially decided to ban it, there was a split. Those who felt hacking was vital to football withdrew from the FA and eventually formed their own rugby leagues.

The game that was agreed on at the meeting became known as association football— a game played according to the rules of the FA. Historian Paul Gardner explains how the term *soccer* came to be: "It was student slang, fond of dropping the end of a word and replacing it with 'er' or 'ers' (e.g. 'brekkers' for breakfast) that coined the two words 'rugger' from Rugby, and 'soccer,' evidently based on the abbreviation Assoc."[12]

Interestingly, however, although the word *soccer* began as English slang, the game was properly referred to as football in England. Today the words are used interchangeably in England, but *soccer* remains a more informal term.

Arriving on British Feet

Having finally agreed to rules for the game, English athletes played soccer in ever-increasing numbers. No longer was it viewed as a brutish, violent game (although it occasionally could be both of those things). Parents cheered on their sons in school matches, and many fans enjoyed watching older players in club games. These fans were so mad

A late nineteenth-century engraving depicts Football Association players.

for their soccer games, in fact, that it seemed quite natural to take the game with them when they journeyed to other places.

While soccer's popularity was growing rapidly in England, the country itself was also growing rapidly into one of the most powerful, important countries of the world. In the late 1800s England was at the height of its political and commercial strength. English businessmen were making deals all over the world, and English sailors left by the thousands to remote ports. England was also a colonial power, with holdings all around the globe. And just as the Roman soldiers had done many centuries before, the English who occupied these lands and did business in their borders brought soccer with them.

It caught on easily in Wales and Scotland, two countries bordering England.

Soccer spread to the continent by way of English students attending German or French boarding schools. And the Italians, who had been playing their own brand of football, called *calcio,* for many years, embraced the new rules as well.

Soccer became popular in South America, starting in Argentina. British sailors and railroad workers (Argentina's railroads were British-owned at the time)

An English and Scottish soccer team battle each other. Scotland and many other countries adopted soccer from the English.

THE LINK BETWEEN AMERICAN SOCCER AND BASEBALL

Since professional soccer leagues have been slow to succeed in the United States, many people might believe that soccer played at a professional level is rather new to this country, but they would be mistaken.

Actually, professional soccer began here in 1894 with the creation of the American League of Professional Football. Europeans were immigrating to the United States in record numbers, and they were bringing their own style of football with them. Therefore, there was a ready supply of fans as well as young men hopeful to make a team.

Interestingly, it was the Eastern Division of the National Baseball League that promoted professional soccer. Baseball officials felt that scheduling soccer games on days when baseball games weren't being played would guarantee that stadiums would be busy more often, generating more profit for them. They hoped that eastern cities such as New York, Baltimore, and Boston would support the new soccer league.

The scheme failed, however. While attendance at the first few games was decent, subsequent afternoon games were sparsely attended often by less than one hundred fans. Had the promoters taken a moment to realize that the bulk of soccer enthusiasts were recent immigrants—blue-collar workers who could not get away for a weekday afternoon soccer game—they might have scheduled things more efficiently. By the time a new league attempted years later to do it right, American football had already become the nation's fall sport of choice.

were playing soccer in their free time in the 1870s. Within a decade, soccer clubs were organized into leagues. Englishmen in Chile, Uruguay, and Brazil soon followed. By the turn of the century, says one historian, soccer had exploded onto the scene in Europe and South America "with all the irresistibility of an idea whose time had come."[13]

In the United States

The same warm welcome was not extended to the game by the United States, however. In the late 1800s there were some schools and colleges that played either the handling or the dribbling game.

But when prestigious schools such as Harvard were asked to join a league for the dribbling game, they refused. Rugby-style football, which was quickly evolving into American-style football, was far more popular, and the soccer leagues faded.

Many experts feel that the rejection of soccer in those days was rooted in the desire to be separate and different from Europe. Those Americans who did play the game were quite frequently recent immigrants from Ireland, Scotland, or England, says historian Bill Murray:

In the United States ties with the homeland had long been cut, and for over a century its citizens had carved out their own destiny. . . . In sport as in other aspects of life, Americans invented their own games: baseball as the popular passion, American football in the colleges, and later basketball. . . . Soccer remained a backwater in the United States, the game of the recent immigrants, and as such one that was frowned on by parents who wanted their sons to become good Americans.[14]

Clearly, it seemed that the innovations in soccer that would take place over the next generation would be made in places other than the United States.

CHAPTER 2

Fine-Tuning the Game

THE MEN WHO gathered at Freemasons' Tavern in London in 1863 came up with a set of rules for soccer; however, the game was still fairly freewheeling. For example, there was no definitive answer as to how many players composed a team; while soccer games no longer involved five hundred or more players at a time (as sometimes occurred in the twelfth century), the numbers of players still greatly varied. Some schools or clubs played with as many as thirty on a side; others played with as few as ten.

As soccer became more and more popular, such inconsistencies were ironed out. The Football Association—and later organizations of a more international nature—turned their attention to making the game better. Some rules were added and others were changed to make soccer more fun to play—as well as more exciting to watch.

Some Basics Have Changed

The early rules set down in London, though clear about hacking the ball (which was forbidden), were not nearly as clear about the basics, particularly the size of the playing field, the size of the ball, or even about the length of the game.

According to those early rules, the field—or "pitch," as it is called in England—could be as long as 200 yards and as wide as 100 yards. Over the years, the field has shrunk; a soccer game today is played on a field the approximate size of a football field, between 100 and 130 yards long and between 50 and 100 yards wide.

Not long after 1863, the goal consisted of a string or belt that was hung between two posts.

The goal was defined in 1863 as "two upright posts, without any tape or bar across them."[15] Not long afterward, players put a string or belt between the goal posts, and a new rule stated that to be considered a goal, the ball had to pass under the string. That is, a ball kicked over the string, which was about eight feet from the ground, did not count as a goal. Eventually, a crossbar replaced both string and belt.

The Ball

A soccer ball in the late 1800s was made of hand-stitched panels of brown leather. The ball would become very heavy if there was even a trace of moisture on the field, and on a rainy day it would triple its weight with the water it absorbed. There were a great many broken ankles and hurt knees from players attempting to kick a waterlogged ball—not to mention the nasty concussions from heading one!

In the nineteenth century the stitched panels of soccer balls were tied together with a length of stiff leather lace—another hazard for a player heading the ball. In 1938 three men from Argentina developed a system to bypass the laces, enclosing the air-filled rubber pouch in smooth leather panels.

The lack of quality leather was sometimes a problem. During World War II soccer balls were frequently made of thin, low-quality leather. There were many matches that were disrupted when a shot on the goal resulted in a burst ball. In the mid-1950s companies made white balls that were far easier for spectators to see. Modern soccer balls are made of high-grade leather and are treated with polyurethane, which prevents water from being absorbed into the panels.

Hands? No Hands?

Next to hacking, the aspect of football that proponents of the dribbling game most wanted to do away with was using the hands to catch the ball. It is surprising, then, that one of the rules put down by the representatives at Freemasons' Tavern in 1863 was that the use of the hands to catch the ball was not banned but only limited.

Any player could catch the ball as long as he put it on the ground immediately afterward and kicked it. He was not permitted to throw the ball forward to another player (as

Stiff leather lace was used to tie together nineteenth-century soccer balls.

was permissible in early rugby matches) or to run with the ball. Even so, the rules permitting any ball handling by players were changed within a few years; only goalkeepers were allowed to handle the ball.

But while some aspects of the game were changed or modified, one key element was not: the object of soccer, which was to score more goals than the opposing team. Any ball that was kicked or headed into the other team's goal counted as a point. When a player kicked in a goal in those early days, he would literally score a notch on the wooden goalpost. The term *score* has stuck, for players are said to "score" goals even though the goalposts are metal or fiberglass and no notch-making is allowed.

At the end of the game's allotted time (which at first could be anywhere from one to three hours, but was soon set at two forty-five-minute halves), the team with the most goals won.

The Scottish Way

Determining the best way to score those goals was the challenge faced by English soccer teams in the late 1800s. Teams had no particular strategy; there were no coaches or trainers to tell players what to do. As soccer enthusiast Eduardo Galeano writes, "In those days no one played a particular position on the field; they all ran happily after the ball, each wherever he wanted, and everyone changed positions at will."[16]

BASIC RULES OF "THE SIMPLEST GAME"

In *The Ultimate Encyclopedia of Soccer: The Definitive Illustrated Guide to World Soccer*, editor Keir Radnedge prints the results of the meeting at Freemasons' Tavern in October 1863. These are the ten chief rules of what the officials there called "the simplest game."

1. A goal is scored whenever the ball is forced through the goal and under the bar, except it be thrown by hand.
2. Hands may be used only to stop a ball and place it on the ground before the feet.
3. Kicks must be aimed only at the ball.
4. A player may not kick the ball whilst in the air.
5. No tripping up or heel kicking allowed.
6. Whenever a ball is kicked beyond the side flags, it must be returned by the player who kicked it, from the spot it passed the flag line, in a straight line towards the middle of the ground.
7. When a ball is kicked behind the line of goal, it shall be kicked off from that line by one of the side whose goal it is.
8. No player may stand within six paces of the kicker when he is kicking off.
9. A player is 'out of play' immediately when he is in front of the ball, and must return behind the ball as soon as possible. If the ball is kicked by his own side past a player, he may not touch or kick it, or advance, until one of the other side has first kicked it, or one of his own side has been able to kick it on a level with, or in front of him.
10. No charging allowed when a player is out of play; that is, immediately the ball is behind him.

These early soccer teams, which comprised eleven players, including a goalkeeper, had one purpose only—to score goals. As soccer expert Bill Murray writes, the only strategy was "to get behind the man with the ball and rush forward in a mighty mass, with the hope of forcing the ball through the goal."[17] As the ball moved around on the field, the players must have looked like a swarm of bees as they followed it, waiting for the player who was dribbling to either lose it or score. No one thought to pass, and no one played defense—except the goalkeeper.

In 1872 the way English players thought about playing soccer changed. It was then that the first international match was played—a championship team from England played the best team from Glasgow, Scotland. The Queen's Park Team, as the Scots were called, demonstrated an entirely new way of playing soccer—passing the ball.

While the English players took turns dribbling the ball with their feet as far as they could toward the Scottish goal before losing the ball, the Scots were more interactive. If the man who was dribbling the ball realized he had nowhere to go with it, or if he saw that a teammate was open nearby, he would pass the ball. The quick, fast passes made by the Scottish players confounded the English; because a hard pass travels faster than a player can run, the English champions could not keep up. The 1872 match, which ended with an easy victory for Queen's Park, was no fluke. Between 1876 and 1885, the Scots defeated the English in eight out of nine challenges.

A Different Kind of Game

As more teams learned from the Scottish teams and began to put more emphasis on passing, the game changed. Soccer became more of a team game, and players learned that, to be effective, they needed to position themselves on the field rather than simply run after the ball.

Besides the goalkeeper, there are three basic positions on the field: defenders, forwards, and midfielders. The defenders' job is to stay back with the goalkeeper, to help prevent goals from being scored. Although they are not permitted to use their hands, defenders are usually fast and quick, with strong legs to clear the ball away when the opposing team threatens.

Forwards are often the fastest members on the team. Their job is to score goals, either by dribbling past the defenders or by making runs into the goal area to be open for a teammate's pass. The midfielders play basically where their name suggests—midway between the defenders and the forwards. They do double duty—passing to the forwards (and scoring goals on occasion) as well as coming back on defense when necessary.

Goalies

Goalkeepers are in a class by themselves, primarily because they play differently than other players. As the last defense of

Goalkeepers require excellent coordination.

their teams' goals, the goalkeepers (often called either "keepers" or "goalies") need more gymnastic ability than traditional soccer skills to do their job. They may leap to catch the ball, or when that is impossible, they may punch or tip it away from the net. Goalies frequently must put themselves in harm's way by diving for balls at the feet of opponents.

Not only do goalkeepers play in a different manner than their teammates, but they dress differently too. To make the goalies stand out, so that they are not confused with a field player when there are many players around the goal, they must wear a color different from either team.

The position of goalkeepers, a difficult position to play, is made more difficult because of the tremendous responsibility involved. Even in the early days of soccer, it was difficult to find a player who wanted to play the goalkeeping position. In his book *Soccer in Sun and Shadow,* Eduardo Galeano sympathetically explains why:

He wears the number one on his back. The first to be paid? No, the first to pay. It's always the keeper's fault. And if it isn't, he still gets blamed. . . . When the team has a bad afternoon, he's the one who pays the bill, expiating the sins of others under a rain of flying balls. The rest of the players can blow it once in awhile, or often, and then redeem themselves with a spectacular dribble, a masterful pass, a

well-placed volley. Not him. The crowd never forgives the keeper.[18]

Paying for Good Players

Soccer's change from a dribbling-only game to one in which passing was used made it more interesting for spectators. The Football Association (FA) continued to sponsor tournaments for English teams as well as championship matches like those played with Scotland. However, there was a problem with the FA's English leagues.

To the teams in the north of England, along Scotland's border, it seemed that the London soccer teams had a distinct advantage. Because the population was largest in the city, there were many more players from which to select a championship team—and the English champions were almost always city teams.

Because of this perceived injustice, some of the teams from the north began to look across the border to Scotland as a resource. Not only were they excellent passers, but the Scots also had remarkable endurance and speed; by having a few Scottish players on their rosters, these northern English teams felt they would have a better chance against the teams from London.

The lure of a job in the mines or in one of England's factories appealed to many poor Scots, and teams who could assure a well-paying job were rewarded with new manpower on the soccer fields. And to

AGAINST PROFESSIONALISM

Included in Tony Mason's book, *Passion of the People? Football in South America* is a quotation by Louis Oestrup, the vice president of FIFA in 1928. Oestrup echoed the feeling of many soccer enthusiasts, who felt that professionalism, if allowed, would ultimately damage the sport.

Professionals are in this respect quite outside the frames of the Football organizations. They are artists, good or bad, such as men generally are. The more you pay them, the more interest they will show, but this has nothing to do with the sport spirit . . . and aim of sport, and it is not for the benefit of artists that countries and towns subsidize sport and numerous people in all countries spend time and work for the interest of Football.

Sportsmen as Professionals are a mistake. Professionals as Artists are the proof of the fact that both leaders and footballers forget the ideals of sport. Sport [is] for every young man in the country, for the health of the nations and not for the purse of some players.

In the 1920s, many enthusiasts believed that professionalism would damage the game.

keep their new players happy, the team secretly paid the imported players after each game. Explains one historian, "A sort of soccer Santa Claus would go round the locker room while the players were bathing, placing money in their boots."[19]

The Professionalism Debate

There was trouble when word leaked out that some players were being paid. The Football Association, which had succeeded in changing the image of the game from one played by street mobs to one played at pricey English boarding schools, was particularly angry. Soccer was to be played by amateurs, for the love of the game, it said. Paid professionals were in shadier sports—such as horse racing and prizefighting—sports that were often connected to illegal activities. This was not supposed to happen with soccer.

The association acted quickly in 1882 after a northern team, the Blackburn Rovers, made it to the finals of the FA Cup, the most prestigious soccer match of the year. The Rovers had at least two "professors," as the paid players were sometimes called—men who had been given jobs in the foundry so that they could play soccer. Blackburn was edged out by a London team, but the FA was taking no chances. The organization's board met immediately after the game and passed a rule that no team with paid players could belong to the FA.

The northern clubs countered with a threat of their own: Unless the FA backed off, they would pull out of the organization and start their own association. In addition, a random investigation by the FA turned up proof that there were "professors" even on most of the city teams. Clearly, it seemed to be a losing battle, and the FA grudgingly withdrew the new rule. Players could be paid; professional soccer had officially begun.

The Birth of the Penalty Kick

Another rule proposed by the Football Association *did* meet with the approval of the teams, however. The violence directly in front of the goal when a team was attacking was becoming more and more pronounced. Knowing that it was a do-or-die situation with the opposing team getting that close to their goal, the defenders of the other team were ruthless. They would punch, kick, elbow—whatever it took to repel the ball's advance. A weekly list of the broken bones and critically injured players was published in the *Westminster Gazette*, and most players seemed to have received their injuries in the eighteen-by-forty-four-foot area in front of the goal.

Of course, the referee could call a foul, but the result—a free kick by the victimized team—seemed like mild compensation. After all, the team had been close to scoring a goal when their players were mauled. A free kick was not enough of a

The penalty kick was invented to discourage rough play in front of the goal.

deterrent to the defense—and the FA agreed.

It established a far more meaningful deterrent: the penalty kick. Instead of the fouled player putting the ball back in play and taking his chances (and his life in his hands) again, the referee could make an important judgment. If the defense commits a foul in the eighteen-by-forty-four-foot goal box, the referee's whistle would

stop the clock. A penalty kick is the call.

The referee steps off twelve yards from the goal line, and places the ball on the grass. The fouled team selects one of its most accurate kickers to go head-to-head with the goalkeeper while the rest of the team stands at least ten yards away to watch.

When the whistle blows, the chosen player kicks the ball, trying to score a goal. Because the goalkeeper is not allowed to move before the ball is kicked, he or she is at a severe disadvantage. Experts say that penalty kicks result in a goal more than 90 percent of the time—a true deterrent against intentional roughness by the defending team.

The Headache of the Offsides Rule

There were a number of modifications that changed soccer from the game it was in 1863; however, in 1925 a rule change occurred that, unlike previous changes, drastically affected the game. The change was to the offsides rule—one of the most basic rules of the game.

The rule originally declared that no offensive player (that is, a player running toward the opposing team's goal) could receive the ball unless there were three opposing players between him and the goal. The idea behind the rule was to prevent a team from just sending one of its players downfield to wait next to the opposing goal. Unless there was a rule preventing it, the player could simply stand there ready to receive a long pass from a teammate—and be in a one-on-one situation with the goalie. And, as explained earlier about penalty kicks, that matchup almost always went in favor of the kicker.

Wanting to prevent such easy scoring opportunities for either team, therefore, the men who decided on the rules back at Freemasons' Tavern in 1863 specified that such long forward passes were illegal unless there were defenders between the goal and the player receiving the pass.

The Trap and Complaints

But defenses had been getting craftier since the mid-1800s, when those rules were written. Some teams, such as Newcastle, had worked out a trick that their defenders often played on opponents' forwards.

When the opposing team began moving downfield toward the goal, one of the Newcastle defenders would hurry upfield, away from the goal rather than moving back to help the goalie. This would leave only the goalie and the other defender back to play defense. And having only those two defenders between the attacking player and the goal was a clear offsides violation. The referee would blow a whistle and award a free kick for Newcastle.

Time and time again the Newcastle defense worked their maneuver, which it called the offside trap. Soon other teams were doing it, too, and instead of a fast-paced game with exciting attacks on the goal, the games were interrupted scores of times by offsides whistles.

The constant stoppages made games dull. If the players were frustrated, the fans were downright furious. By 1925 it was commonplace for there to be thirty of forty offsides calls and plenty of low-scoring games.

THE ROOTS OF WOMEN'S SOCCER

In 1972 the United States approved a measure known as Title IX, which introduced the notion of gender equity into college sports. But women and girls have been playing soccer for far longer than that. In fact, the beginnings of women's soccer go back almost as far as the beginnings of the game itself.

Although they were certainly the exception, a few women presumably did join in the mob football games in early England; however, there are no accurate records to prove it. Scottish historians from the late nineteenth century describe matches between single and married women at Inverness. This competition gradually became a regular event in Scotland, although it was the only official women's competition in the world at that time.

Women's soccer got a boost during World War I, when men's leagues were suspended. Young women held charity soccer games to raise money for the Red Cross—some of which were quite well attended. However, after the war, England clamped down on women's sports, and the Football Association voted to ban women from all soccer grounds.

However, some nations were willing to support soccer for young women, including Italy, France, and the United States, where girls' soccer was catching on at the high school level. Eventually England came around, lifting its earlier ban in 1970. Since that time women's soccer has grown steadily throughout the world, especially with the beginning of the Women's World Cup in 1991.

An 1895 drawing shows nineteenth-century women competing in a game of soccer.

A Change for the Better

Clearly something had to be done, and in 1925 the offsides rule was changed. Beginning immediately, an attacking player needed only two defenders between himself and the goal.

Although this perhaps does not sound like much of a change, it had a dramatic effect on the game. For one thing, defenses were less likely to try the offsides trap because it was far more risky. If something went wrong under the old system—say, the referee failed to notice the offsides violation or the move was mistimed—there was still a defender back with the goalie to keep the ball out of the net. But under this new system, if the trap didn't work, the goalkeeper was defenseless.

Predictably, there were fewer defensive offside traps attempted and, therefore, fewer offsides calls by the referees. And the low-scoring games almost overnight became a thing of the past. Goals were up more than 40 percent the following season in the English leagues, and fans were thrilled.

The Defense Strikes Back

But the new offsides rule had a more far-ranging effect. Without the offside trap to rely on, teams were forced to rethink the tactics that they had been using. Up until 1925, most teams played what was called a 2-3-5 alignment. That is, there were two defenders (besides the goalkeeper); three midfielders, whose main focus was setting up goals for the forwards; and the five offensive forwards.

Scoring increased after soccer's offsides rule was changed in 1925.

The English Arsenal team, led by coach Herbert Chapman, was the first to alter this field arrangement. The team noticed that the center forward was the player who scored most of the goals on teams. By neutralizing that position, Chapman reasoned, he could lessen the amount of scoring being done with the new offsides rule.

He and the team captain, Charlie Buchan, devised a new system. They dropped the center midfielder back to defense so that three defenders were in front of the goalkeeper. This new defender's job would be to guard, or "mark," the opposing center forward. This position was often called "the policeman" or "the stopper." The hole at midfield could be filled in with one of the forwards dropping back, if necessary.

This new alignment, usually called the 3-4-3, was considered quite unusual at first; however, by the end of the 1926 season almost all teams had adopted some variation of it. Although the forwards were still scoring more easily than in the past, the defenders were rapidly making progress in stopping the onslaught of balls flying into the net—all to the delight of the ever-increasing numbers of soccer fans around the world.

CHAPTER 3

The Changing Face of Soccer

IN ITS BEGINNINGS, soccer was a mob sport played by commoners in England. However, by the time it was organized and its rules were written down, the sport was played by the privileged segment of society: the young men at prestigious schools and colleges. But by the end of the nineteenth century, this had changed—and with this change, the entire face of the game would change too.

The Power of the Working Man

Professionalism profoundly shifted the demographics of soccer. The first Scottish emigrants who were lured to England to play soccer were not well educated or from wealthy families. But their talent on the soccer field made them valuable assets to the growing number of soccer teams in England.

With the Football Association's begrudging permission for English clubs to go professional, the door was open for other men from humble beginnings to make money as athletes. Young athletes could dream of making money by sheer physical talent—something almost unheard of in those days. And by the late 1800s, over one hundred clubs in England, Scotland, and Wales were eager for such talent—no matter how much money the players' families had. It was in this way that the game passed from the hands of privileged members of British society to those of the common people.

Soccer quickly became a game played—and watched—by the working class as well as the privileged. Leagues were formed in small mining and industrial towns, and local boys sharpened their skills in hope that they might someday be chosen for a major team.

This newfound enthusiasm had a very visible effect on their communities. A midweek game between two local clubs could bring a factory or mill to a complete standstill as workers left early to watch the game. "As much as the bosses might rage about this," writes one expert, "there was nothing they could do about it. The hills around Barley Bank [near Lancashire] were black with people enjoying not only an afternoon off work but also a free view of the game from the outside of the enclosure."[20]

British Arrogance

Soccer had become popular in South America in the late nineteenth century, as British merchants and entrepreneurs had set up operations in Argentina, Uruguay, and Brazil. Leagues there had been set up only for these businessmen and their families at first. However, the face of South American soccer was changing despite resistance by the British who first introduced the sport.

In the late nineteenth century, for example, the British population in Buenos Aires, Argentina, was four hundred thousand. These Brits were railroad executives, bankers, and the heads of the meatpacking industry, and they composed the top economic bracket. And because they had no interest in mingling with the

A nineteenth-century drawing depicts boys practicing soccer in the hopes that they will someday play professionally.

CALCIO

During the late nineteenth century, soccer found its way to Italy. However, as Paul Gardner writes in *SoccerTalk: Life Under the Spell of the Round Ball*, Italian football, known as "calcio," was far from English-style soccer.

The Italian climate and the Italian temperament produced a new version of the sport. The biggest influence on Italian soccer, or *calcio*, was to come indirectly from Scotland. The Scots had developed a game that, while incorporating all the elements of English soccer, was distinguished by its reliance on short, on-the-ground passing plays. The style caught on in Austria and Hungary, and by the 1920s the Italians had seen enough of it to know that it suited them too.

Calcio became a game with a larger dose of artistry than English soccer, a game with less emphasis on strength and more on ball control. Tackling was less evident in *calcio*, in which a good team gained possession more as the result of interceptions than by physically dispossessing an opponent. *Calcio* also had an acrobatic quality, a touch of Italian bravura, that the English shunned in their own game, suspicious as they have always been of anything that looks like exhibitionism.

The overall pace of *calcio* is certainly slower than that of the English game; the Italians have always professed admiration at the ability of the English players to run inexhaustibly for the full 90 minutes of a game.

Argentine people, the Englishmen and their families had their own schools, churches, colleges, two daily newspapers—and several thriving soccer clubs.

Gradually some of the wealthier Argentine merchants and businessmen started their own teams, although the Argentine Football Association was completely British-run. There were rules, for example, that were in effect only because of the British. No Spanish could be spoken at meetings, for instance, and because England never held matches on Sundays, that carried over to the Argentine players as well. Games were held on Saturday, without question.

"To Play Well and Without Passion"

Above all, the soccer that was played in places like Argentina, Brazil, and Uruguay—even when it was played by the native people themselves—was firmly entrenched in the British model. As one expert notes, when examining the soccer in South America in the late nineteenth and early twentieth centuries, "What seems clear is that they tried to uphold what they considered to be British ideas of fair play, 'to play well and without passion,' and certainly to avoid unseemly conflicts on the field."[21]

Modesty on the field was a British tradition at the turn of the century. While soccer players of today wear shorts and loose-fitting jerseys, British soccer players in those days considered it in bad taste to dress so scantily, even in very hot temperatures.

"Old photographs show these pioneers in sepia tones," explains one historian. "They were warriors trained for battle. Cotton and wool almost covered their entire bodies so as not to offend the ladies in attendance, who unfurled silk parasols and waved lace handkerchiefs."[22] The Argentine merchants and businessmen who played soccer dressed the same way, although short pants would have been far more suitable to their way of thinking. Wool soccer pants and shirts were ordered from England.

"The Playing of Sports Is Becoming an Agony"

Rather than feel proud that the game they had brought to South America was being embraced by the people there, many Englishmen were irritated. Back in England, some purists were furious that soccer was even being played in foreign lands. Sniffed one Englishman in 1912, "Soccer is not a sport that can hope to flourish in a subtropical climate like that of Brazil."[23]

Those Englishmen who were playing in South America showed more than a little arrogance as well. Even though their own soccer clubs were not "integrated" with South American players, they sometimes

were scheduled to play against Argentine, Brazilian, or Uruguayan teams, and this angered them. They wanted their own leagues so that they could play only other Englishmen, but that wasn't always possible.

The British editor of *Sport!* magazine in Rio de Janeiro complained in 1915 about the fact that more and more British teams were being asked to play against Brazilian teams. The experience, he believed, greatly reduced the enjoyment of the sport. "Those of us who have a certain

Early soccer players were required to wear uncomfortable uniforms.

position in society," he wrote, "are obliged to play with workers, with drivers. . . . The playing of sports is becoming an agony, a sacrifice, never a diversion."[24]

If the English in South America were squeamish playing with the sons of wealthy natives, what would they think about the growing interest shown by some of the continent's poorest young people toward this new game? One wealthy British citizen thought he was seeing things in 1914 when he rode through part of Rio de Janeiro and saw an impromptu soccer game in progress. "The match was between junior teams of about eighteen to twenty years of age," the astonished man wrote to a friend back home. "They were all . . . as black as your hat, and most of them playing in bare feet."[25] Little did he realize that he was seeing the future of the game.

"Skillful Blending of Brains and Boots"

As soccer grew in popularity among the working people of Brazil, Argentina, and Uruguay, English teams began making the long journey (by boat) to play local teams. Southampton, one of the finest professional teams in England, came to Buenos Aires in 1904 to play several matches.

The very fact that a professional team had come such a long way to play was exciting in itself; however, the skill that Southampton showed as it easily defeated the local teams greatly impressed the thousands of spectators who came to watch. Even twenty years later, local fans and players were marveling over the one-sidedness of the contests as well as Southampton's "magnificent work with head and feet, their skillful blending of brains and boots."[26]

For the British, the experience certainly confirmed their idea that no matter who learned the game, they themselves would always dominate. For the Argentines—and for the Brazilians and Uruguayans, who also had opportunities to play English teams—it was a chance to learn by seeing the best in the world.

A New Brand of Soccer

But as the observer in Rio de Janeiro noted in 1914, it was not only the South American workers and merchants who were learning about soccer. Excitement about the game was trickling down to the youngest—and poorest—of the South American people.

The process, notes Uruguayan writer Eduardo Galeano, was inevitable—and unstoppable: "Like the tango, soccer blossomed in the slums. It required no money and could be played with nothing more than sheer desire. In fields, in alleys, and on beaches, native-born kids and young immigrants improvised games using balls made of old socks filled with rags or paper, and a couple of stones for a goal."[27]

Many of these new soccer players were mulatto or black, people who had very lit-

The Southampton players (striped jerseys) defeated their opponents with their impressive skills.

tle political or economic clout in their countries. But such things had nothing to do with their creativity with the ball. It was in the ghettos of the big cities of Argentina, Uruguay, and particularly Brazil that a new style of soccer was born.

Whereas the English style of soccer relied on strength, force, and an exquisite ability to head the ball, the smaller, slighter ghetto youths of Brazil invented their own style of play. Unable to dominate by leaping for headers or taking the ball from opponents by force, these players let the ball bounce on their chests and down to their feet, where they could dribble rings around almost anyone else. It was full of surprises, says one expert, "full of changes of pace—sudden sprints followed by periods when their immaculate ball control allowed the Brazilians to slow the game down to a walk."[28]

It was, soccer enthusiasts today agree, the most beautiful soccer style in the

RACISM IN SOCCER

Even though sports are not political, they have always reflected the attitudes and biases of society. Just as black players were unwelcome for many years in American major league baseball, black and mulatto players were banned from soccer in Brazil for a time, as Eduardo Galeano explains in *Soccer in Sun and Shadow.*

In 1921 the South American Cup was played in Buenos Aires. The president of Brazil . . . issued a decree: for reasons of patriotic prestige there would be no brown skin on Brazil's national team. . . .

Friedenreich [a mulatto soccer star] did not play in that championship tournament. It was impossible to be black in Brazilian soccer, and being mulatto wasn't easy either. Friedenreich always started late because it took him half an hour to iron his hair in the dressing room. The only mulatto player on Fluminence [one of Brazil's professional teams], Carlos Alberto, used to whiten his face with rice powder.

Later on, despite the owners of power, things began to change. With the passage of time, the old soccer mutilated by racism gave way to the splendor of its diverse colors. And after so many years it is obvious that Brazil's best players . . . have always been blacks and mulattos. All of them came up from poverty, and some of them returned to it. By contrast, there have never been blacks or mulattos among Brazil's car-racing champions. Like tennis, it is a sport that requires money.

world, more like dancing than a game, a sport "made of hip feints, undulations of the torso and legs in flight, all of which came from *capoeira,* the warrior dance of black slaves, and from the joyful dances of the big-city slums."[29]

How would teams made up of these youths do against traditional British teams? It would be years before such interaction would take place.

FIFA

It was not just in South America that soccer was gaining momentum. Soccer leagues in many European nations were highly successful. And although they, too, had been unable to beat English teams in a match whenever an opportunity presented itself, the number of young players learning the game was promising.

It is not surprising, then, that there was soon talk in Europe of creating an international soccer foundation. Such an organization could oversee the game throughout the world and, as the Football Association in England had done, could make certain that there was consistency in the rules from one country to the next.

In 1904 representatives of seven nations—Holland, Belgium, Denmark, Switzerland, Spain, Sweden, and France—met in Paris to discuss founding such an organization. They called the new organization the Federation Internationale de Football Association (FIFA).

Join? Quit?

The other nations hoped that England would be a part of FIFA; its experience and leadership would undoubtedly prove helpful. But English representatives did not attend the planning meeting. At that time Great Britain had what was called the International Board, and it governed soccer in England, Wales, Ireland, and Scotland. Therefore, it did not believe that another international regulatory organization was necessary.

Besides, FIFA's "one nation, one vote" policy rankled British soccer officials. Why should the country that made the rules for the game—not to mention exporting it to foreign lands—be limited to a single vote? Within two years, however, England conceded. FIFA agreed to give Great Britain four votes by allowing separate votes for England, Ireland, Wales, and Scotland.

Austria, Germany, Italy, and Hungary joined at the same time. The organization grew steadily; Canada, Chile, and Argentina joined in 1912, and the United States joined the following year. It seemed as though the idea of an international soccer organization finally had caught on.

The Olympics

One of the dreams of the founders of FIFA was to hold a true international competi-

tion for all of the member nations. In fact, when FIFA started in 1904, one of the first proclamations it made was that it alone had the authority to structure and run a world soccer tournament. But another organization—the International Olympic Committee (IOC)—beat FIFA to it in 1908.

The concept of national teams had always intrigued soccer-playing countries. And although the IOC had never considered having soccer as an event in the Olympic Games, it was decided that for the 1908 games, held in London, soccer would be an official sport.

Five nations were able to assemble teams that year, and to no one's surprise, England won the gold medal by beating Denmark in the final match by a score of 2-0. Four years later, eleven nations competed in soccer at the Olympic Games in Stockholm, Sweden. Again, England dominated play, beating the Danes in the final.

War and a Demand

Competitive international soccer was put on hold—as were all international sporting events—during World War I. Historians say, however, that although the Olympics were canceled during that time, soccer was still being played. In fact, writes one expert, soccer games were going on "behind the trenches in Europe, in the lulls between artillery barrages, and on

Although World War I overshadowed sports, some soldiers played soccer behind the trenches during lulls in fighting.

one famous occasion in no-man's land, where combatants played during the first Christmas truce."[30]

But if people thought that the cooperative spirit within FIFA would continue after the war ended in 1918, they were sadly mistaken. England, France, and Belgium were still angry with Germany because of the war, and they formally demanded that Germany and its allies be removed from the association. But FIFA disagreed, saying that politics needed to stay out of international sports. As a result, England furiously withdrew from FIFA; Belgium

and France reconsidered their position on the issue and remained.

The Argument over Professionalism

The 1924 Olympics were held in Paris and were a definite turning point for international soccer. Earlier in the year, Great Britain had again switched its position and had returned to FIFA. Since the war had been over for nearly six years, it seemed foolish to British representatives to continue boycotting the association. However, there was a problem almost immediately, and it concerned an issue that had at one time greatly troubled British soccer: professionalism.

The Olympics have always been a contest for amateur athletes, those who play for the love of the sport. Players who were paid had never been eligible to take part on their national Olympic team. When soccer first was played as an Olympic sport, professionalism wasn't an issue since Great Britain was the only nation with paid players. There were plenty of excellent amateur players in the country, so there was no trouble fielding an Olympic team.

But by 1924, there were several nations that had professional teams and leagues. And unlike England, which had an abundance of excellent amateur players, many of these other countries did not. More and more highly talented players from impoverished backgrounds—particularly in South America—were learning that soccer could be a ticket out of poverty.

FIFA, which handled Olympic soccer, realized it was important for the sport and the spectators to keep the level of play high. To ban most of the best European and South American players because they were paid in their countries seemed unfair and counterproductive, for they were some of the most entertaining to watch. Therefore, a deal was struck with the IOC for the 1924 Olympic Games. The top players from nations could compete, even if they had been paid in the past.

But this decision angered the British representatives, who thought it represented "a breach of the true spirit of amateurism."[31]

The opening day ceremony of the 1924 Olympic Games, soccer's Olympic debut.

And because FIFA refused to change its decision about allowing these players to participate, the four representatives from Great Britain again left FIFA. This time it would not return for almost twenty years.

"We Are No Longer Just a Tiny Spot on the Map"

The soccer world was buzzing over the absence of Great Britain at the 1924 Olympics, held in the Netherlands; as the only gold-medal winner since the sport was included in the Olympic Games, Great Britain had always set a high stan-dard for other teams. But who would win the gold that year?

As it turned out, it was tiny Uruguay, a country that did not even have the money to pay for its team's passage to Paris. (Some of Uruguay's wealthy citizens had donated money so that the team could participate, one even mortgaged his house to help defray the cost of the trip.) It was the first time a Latin American team had ever played in Europe; no European nation even considered that Uruguay could win a match, let alone the gold medal.

The team was a ragtag group of players, almost all of whom were from the poor

A portrait of the 1924 Uruguay World Cup soccer team.

working class. One Uruguayan writer describes the team:

> Pedro Arispe was a meat-packer. Jose Nasazzi cut marble. Perucho Petrone worked for a grocer. Pedro Cea sold ice. Jose Leandro Andrade was a carnival musician and a bootblack. They were all twenty years old, more or less, though in the pictures they look like senior citizens. They cured their wounds with salt water, vinegar plasters and a few glasses of wine.[32]

But Uruguay stunned the fifty thousand spectators who crowded into a French stadium for the final match by beating Switzerland 3-0. Many Uruguayans felt that winning the Olympic medal had finally gotten their country noticed. Said one proud Uruguayan, "We are no longer just a tiny spot on the map of the world."[33]

The Need for a New Tournament

While FIFA had been successful in its attempts to allow professional players to compete in the 1924 Olympics, the IOC decided it was a bad precedent to set. From here on out, it announced, only amateur athletes would be allowed to compete—even in soccer.

However, this decision had interesting consequences. With bans against professional players, Olympic soccer was not going to maintain the high level of play that had excited the spectators in the past, particularly in 1924. And since the best players were not eligible to play in the Olympics, another tournament had to be created to accommodate them.

A French representative to FIFA, Henri Delaunay, explained in 1926 at the yearly FIFA conference, "Today international football can no longer be held within the confines of the Olympics; and many countries where professionalism is now recognized and organized cannot any longer be represented there by their best players."[34]

Others agreed with Delaunay, particularly Frenchman Jules Rimet, who had been elected president of FIFA in 1921. Rimet had enthusiastically campaigned for a FIFA tournament of this sort during the 1924 Olympics, and he was eager for the organization to create one.

The World Cup

Experts say that Delaunay and Rimet were a perfect match when it came to accomplishing their goal of creating the international tournament; their personalities complemented one another. "Between them," notes soccer expert Paul Gardner, "building on their experience in organizing soccer within France, these two provided exactly the right combination of vision, coaxing, arm-twisting, and ruthlessness necessary to transmute their dream into reality."[35]

Delaunay urged FIFA to sponsor a true international championship for soccer, and his motion was voted on and passed. It was decided that the tournament, called the World Cup, would be held every four years, just as the Olympics were. But to ensure that the two events did not interfere with one another, the World Cup would begin in 1930 (in a year when the Olympic Games did not take place).

Several countries volunteered to host the first World Cup, among them Italy, the Netherlands, Spain, and Sweden. However, it was Uruguay who was given the honor. As the winner of the past two Olympic soccer gold medals (the Uruguayan national team had won again in 1928) Uruguay seemed a good choice. Besides that, the nation would be celebrating its one hundredth year of independence in 1930, and that would coincide nicely with a World Cup.

The European nations were aghast by the decision; how could such a small country host such a large event? Uruguay did not even have a large enough stadium for a final match that would attract tens of thousands of spectators.

But Uruguay, eager to be the host, promised FIFA two things: It would build a massive one hundred thousand-seat stadium in the capital city of Montevideo, and it would pay every team's full expenses to make the trip. In the end FIFA agreed, and Uruguay set to work building its new stadium.

However, the reaction of the rest of the FIFA members made it clear that relations within the organization would be far from harmonious. Many nations refused to make the three-week boat trip to Uruguay, no matter how little the journey cost. After all, the travel expenses would only help the nations that sent the teams, not the players themselves. Being gone almost two months would mean a great deal of lost wages.

Europe's dissatisfaction with FIFA's decision was evident as the tournament grew near. The nations with the mightiest soccer teams—Germany, Austria, Czechoslovakia, Hungary, Italy, Spain, and Switzerland—refused to enter the competition. Great Britain was still feuding with FIFA over professionalism, and it was not even a member. It was not a promising picture for the first-ever World Cup.

Successful Nonetheless

France, too, was reluctant to attend, although the very fact that two Frenchmen had lobbied hard for the tournament made its appearance necessary. Besides, Uruguay had made the trip to Paris for the Olympic Games in 1924, so France would lose face if it failed to reciprocate.

In the end, France agreed to participate, and it was followed by three other European nations: Romania, Belgium, and, at the last moment, Yugoslavia. None of these countries, except France, was much of a threat to win the tournament, however. The Americas, on the other hand, were well represented. Besides Uruguay, seven South

Argentina's goalie dives in vain during the 1930 World Cup final.

American nations entered. Mexico and the United States sent teams also.

Even though things did not look optimistic at first, the 1930 World Cup was a success—especially for the home team. Uruguay advanced easily to the finals, as did Argentina. And in a packed stadium of over ninety thousand people, Uruguay defeated its neighbor 4-2. Remarks one historian, it was so crowded, "there wasn't room for a pin in the stands."[36]

Finally, a tournament had been held that allowed the best athletes to perform, regardless of their professional status. Uruguayans were ecstatic. "The absence of the strongest European countries rendered the title somewhat suspect," notes Paul Gardner, "but the Uruguayan celebrations demonstrated that they had no doubts at all."[37]

Bigger and Bigger

If nothing else, the 1930 World Cup demonstrated to the soccer-playing nations that such an event could indeed be held. Plans were begun almost immediately afterward for the next one, scheduled for 1934.

The World Cup has continued every four years since then, with two exceptions: 1942 and 1946, due to World War II. The tournament has grown, too; no longer is the World Cup held with only thirteen participating teams. Currently there are more than 170 nations who belong to FIFA, and they vie to be participants in the tournament.

The host nation, as well as the nation who won the year before, are automatic qualifiers. The other twenty-two participating teams must win a series of games to qualify. And because of the large number of nations in FIFA, qualifying matches must begin two full years before the World Cup.

The World Cup has provided fans around the world with a great deal of exciting soccer. The tournament's influence is powerful; the hope of someday playing in a World Cup match is the goal of many a soccer player. But the game of soccer has been influenced even more by individual players—those whose skill, sleight, and speed have been emulated and imitated by young players. Whether practicing with their teams or juggling a ball on their feet in the backyard, many players work hard, dreaming of becoming the next great soccer legend.

CHAPTER 4

The Game's Finest

Since its rules were formulated back in 1863 in an English pub, the game of soccer has grown to astronomical proportions. Many skilled and gifted players since then—from many nations around the world—have added their own special mark to the game. But no one has ever come close to the level of play and commitment to the game as the man whose name has become synonymous with soccer: Pelé.

While a star is someone whose abilities are at a far higher level than the average player, soccer fan and former secretary of state Henry Kissinger explains, Pelé was far beyond that. "Pelé's performance transcended that of the ordinary star," Kissinger says, "by as much as the star exceeds ordinary performance." [38]

From the Humblest of Beginnings

He was born Edson Arantes do Nascimento in the incredibly poor town of Tres Coracoes, Brazil, in 1940. He was nicknamed "Dico" by his friends; the name "Pelé," the meaning of which is unknown, was given to him by his soccer friends—but he insists he never liked it. Ironically, Pelé is the name by which he became famous on the soccer field.

Pelé grew up kicking a ball—or a can, a bunch of rags bound up with string or tape, or anything else he could kick. He and his teammates—none of whom could afford shoes—called themselves "the Shoeless Ones."

Without soccer cleats or even tennis shoes, however, Pelé was a formidable

Pelé (right) quickly became one of the game's legends.

brought Pelé to the directors of a professional team called Santos. De Brito told them, "This boy will be the greatest soccer player in the world."[39] Pelé was given a spot on the Santos team, making about sixty dollars per month. The skinny fifteen-year-old did well in his early matches, and soon he was scoring more goals than anyone else on the team. His first year he scored sixty-five goals—a team record.

To the World Cup

Pelé was chosen to be a part of Brazil's 1958 World Cup team, although it was assumed that he wouldn't play much. There were a host of well-known stars on the team, and no one thought the seventeen-year-old was likely to push any of them out of the lineup.

player. His father, Dondinho, had played soccer for a time, but a fractured leg ended his career at an early age. Dondinho hoped his son would achieve the success that he himself had not.

Pelé's father must have been very proud when his son, at age eleven, was noticed by one of Brazil's premier players, Waldemar de Brito. De Brito was amazed at the boy's quickness and touch on the ball. He kept in contact with Pelé and his family, and four years later he

Pelé sat on the bench for the first two games; a pregame warmup had made his right knee very sore. But there was some dissension on the team, and some of the starting players were replaced for the third game. Pelé, cleared by the team doctor, was put into the lineup as a forward against the Soviet Union. Within four minutes he had scored a goal with a blistering shot. He got the assist (passed to the player who scored) in the next goal, and Brazil won 2-0.

From then on, Pelé was in the starting lineup for the remaining World Cup matches. It was in the semifinal game against France that Pelé showed that he could be a leader as well as a powerful scorer. When France tied the game, scoring the first goal Brazil had given up in the tournament, Pelé took charge, as one onlooker reports:

Pelé grabbed the ball out of the net and sprinted back upfield for the restart. There were still 81 minutes left to play, and here was this teenager acting like a quarterback in a two-minute drill. "Let's go! Let's get started! Let's quit wasting time!" he shouted, waving his elder teammates into position. They stared at him, and then, together, they scored the next four goals, three of them by Pelé.[40]

He seemed to be the spark that Brazil needed; the Brazilians beat Sweden in the final game of the World Cup 5-2. Now a permanent member of the starting lineup, Pelé had shown that the rumors circulating about his amazing skills were all true.

Playing with Joy

Many of South America's best players had found their way to European professional teams, where the pay was much higher.

Pelé (no. 10) celebrates with teammates after scoring the winning goal for Brazil in the 1958 World Cup final.

Pelé had offers to go to one of the best Italian teams, but he declined. He loved Brazil, and he would not leave Santos, the team that gave him his first chance to play professionally.

His accomplishments on the soccer field continued, and he seemed to find new ways to dazzle spectators and opponents with each new game. He had a host of nicknames, but none of them did him justice. As one reporter explains, "He was called Gasoline for his energy, the Executioner for his finishing, the Black Pearl for his preciousness."[41] Opposing players knew they were going against the best whenever Pelé was on the field. Said one sports commentator, "When you have Pelé in the team you start with a 2-0 advantage. What point is there in talking of tactics when that madman is on the field?"[42]

Pelé played not only with youthful enthusiasm and determination but also with joy. A marvelous play was to be applauded, whether it was done by him, a teammate, or even by a member of the opposing team. In a match against England in the 1970 World Cup, Pelé had sent a rocketing header toward goalie Gordon Banks—a sure score, it seemed, for Brazil. In what witnesses later said was the best save ever, Banks threw his body across the goal and managed to deflect the shot. In gleeful appreciation of Banks's play, Pelé led the applause for the English goalie.

Pelé embodied the type of exciting, acrobatic soccer that Brazil had become known for, but he also played with a style all of his own. According to soccer expert Paul Gardner,

> What Pelé did, he did in a way that only Pelé could, stamped with his own personality—there was character there, unmistakable, inimitable. That explosive, darting figure, such an impossible combination of ferocious muscular power and delicate, subtle artistry, those sinuous, feline dribbles, the whiplash headers, the thunderbolt shots—the unforgettable excitement of the climactic leap and that triumphant punch at the air.[43]

So Many Records

During his career, Pelé was beloved by not only his millions of Brazilian fans but also by soccer enthusiasts the world over. By the time he was in his mid-twenties, he was the most recognized sports figure on the planet. He was also the highest paid: In 1966 he was making an annual salary of $2 million, which was unheard of in those times.

And everywhere Pelé played, people flocked to the stadium to watch—to see soccer played on a new level. He once even held up a war: In 1967, when he was scheduled to play a match in Lagos, the capital of Nigeria, a forty-eight-hour cease-fire between Nigeria and Biafra was signed so that soldiers and rebels could watch him play.

His career in Brazil was astonishing. In a sport where a player is considered a superstar when he scores fifty goals in a season, Pelé scored one hundred goals in three different seasons. And while a career total of 400 goals is considered amazing, Pelé amassed 1,284 goals in his total of 1,362 matches played.

"Another Mountain to Climb"

When he was thirty-three, Pelé retired from his Santos team. However, within a year he had found a new soccer challenge—one that baffled soccer players around the world. He decided to accept a $4.5-million, three-year deal with a U.S. team: the New York Cosmos.

The Cosmos were a part of the North American Soccer League (NASL), an at-tempt by soccer enthusiasts in the United States to increase awareness and appreciation of the sport. Unfortunately, the league had not caught on as quickly as promoters had hoped. There were many die-hard fans, but not enough to fill stadiums around the country.

Pelé's decision surprised many people; they wondered why the greatest soccer player of all time would want to waste his time playing in a country that was apathetic about the game. The United States was, they reminded him, the only country in the world where he would not be recognized! His answer was simple: "I looked and saw another mountain to climb," he said.[44]

Putting the United States on the Soccer Map

Pelé's dream was to show the U.S. public the game he so dearly loved. He hoped that by seeing soccer played as it should be played—by skilled, creative players—more young people would be inspired to take up the game.

The statistics show that he was very successful. While the pre-Pelé Cosmos (as well as other NASL teams) were playing in front of four-digit crowds, the stadiums filled when Pelé came to town. In addition, the number of soccer players registered with the U.S. Soccer Federation increased fivefold, from one hundred thousand in 1975 to five hundred thousand in 1978. And Pelé's arrival in the

Pelé increased the popularity of soccer in the United States when he played for the New York Cosmos.

United States had sparked other European stars to join the NASL as well, including the famous German star Franz Beckenbauer.

One of the most moving moments in Pelé's time with the Cosmos occurred when his old Brazilian team, Santos, arrived for a match in New York in 1977. The game was sold out—something that had never before happened at a U.S. soccer match—six weeks beforehand.

Pelé played the first half for the Cosmos; the second half he put on the Santos jersey and played for them. He scored for each team, as seventy-five thousand fans shouted and cheered. "It seems that God brought me to Earth with a mission," he wrote later in the *New York Times,* "to unite people, never to separate them."[45]

"The Wizard of Dribble"

But while there has been only one Pelé, there have certainly been other soccer players who have done great things on the soccer field, contributing mightily to the game. One of the best was an Englishman named Stanley Matthews, the first soccer player ever to be knighted.

Matthews was one of a vast number of athletes whose best years were swallowed up by World War II. He was a young man playing on the Stoke City professional team when the war broke out. Matthews joined the Royal Air Force, leaving his soccer career behind.

Stanley Matthews was known for his deft ball control.

No one can possibly know what he might have accomplished if he had been allowed to develop as a player in normal circumstances. But even with a several-year gap in his professional career, Matthews was a superb player who could run right through a defense with deft ball control. For this reason, he was known as "the Wizard of Dribble."

Leaving Opponents in the Dust

Matthews seemed to move the ball effortlessly. Playing right wing, he would dribble until he was almost face to face with the fullback—no more than a yard or two away. Then, leaning to the inside, as though he were going that direction, Matthews would quickly shift his weight and dash to the outside, streaking up the sideline with the ball.

One fellow Englishman recalls watching Matthews make the same move over and over, with the same results. It did not seem to matter, he says, that everyone on the field knew what was going to happen:

And because you knew what was coming, precisely because you knew as soon as Stan got the ball what he was going to do, there was always excitement and anticipation in the air. Shuffle, shuffle, tap, tap—and Stan was suddenly on top of the fullback. Sometimes the action would stop right there for what seemed like ages, the defender almost paralyzed with caution, until Stan decided it was time to sweep by him and on to the goal line. At other times, Stan would take pity and administer the coup immediately. Frequently, the fullback was left sitting on his rear.[46]

Sir Stanley

Matthews had a long career, playing professionally for thirty-three years. He stayed with a very mediocre Stoke City team up until the war began. He had hoped to leave the team and try his luck in a new environment, but he was persuaded to change his plans. The local fans were determined to keep him there. More than three thousand of them stormed the town hall while another thousand stood outside waving signs that read "Matthews Must Not Go."

Matthews stayed at Stoke City for nine more years; after the war, in 1947, he was transferred to Blackpool, where he played the rest of his career—well into his forties. He was named Footballer of the Year in

Stanley Matthews (left) played for the Stoke City and Blackpool teams during his thirty-three-year career.

England in 1956 and again in 1963—a tremendous honor and doubly satisfying for a man whose teammates were younger than his own son. As Eduardo Galeano quips, "When he was fifty years old, Stanley Matthews still caused serious outbreaks of hysteria in British soccer. There weren't enough psychiatrists to deal with all the victims, who had been perfectly normal until the moment they were bewitched by this grandfatherly tormentor of fullbacks."[47]

As a final tribute, Matthews was knighted by Queen Elizabeth in 1965, making him the first soccer player ever to achieve such an honor.

The Great Bobby Moore

Most of the superstars of soccer have been forwards, esteemed for their hard shots and the number of goals they put into the net. Bobby Moore, another English player, specialized in stopping goals, either as a defender or as a defensive midfielder.

He was born in 1941 in London, during the middle of the German blitz on that city. His was from a poor working-class neighborhood, and the hope of most of his friends was to gain a spot on a professional soccer team. That was Moore's dream, too, however, when some of his classmates were called on by professional teams, he started to worry that he would not be chosen. "I was choked," he said later, "when the time came for me to leave school. All my mates had gone off for tri-

Skill and confidence made Bobby Moore one of soccer's greatest defenders.

als with clubs around London but nobody seemed to want me."[48]

Nonetheless, a local club called West Ham gave him a try, and Moore seized the opportunity. He played on what amounted to a farm team for West Ham until 1958, until he turned professional. He would stay with West Ham almost all of his career.

Unflappable

Moore's style was quite different from that of many English players, who usually relied on brawn and sliding tackles to strip an opponent of the ball. Moore was quick and clean, and he used a great sense of timing to sneak the ball away from a dribbler. After that, he would make a quick long pass to a teammate streaking for the goal. Many West Ham goals were scored on just such plays.

His unflappable demeanor on the field helped his less experienced teammates settle down too. Those who played with him say that he never lost his composure on the field. As one West Ham player said,

You can swear at him, kick him, and if you're feeling in a particularly sour mood, take the mickey out of his golden-boy image, but you would still be struggling to get a . . . reaction from him. When the coach gives him instructions, he listens in that composed, matter-of-fact way of his, and if he nods his head that's as much as you can expect.[49]

The 1966 World Cup

Coaches, too, appreciated Moore's dedication and calm nature. As England prepared for

Bobby Moore proudly displays the Jules Rimet trophy after his team's victory in the 1966 World Cup final.

JOHAN CRUYFF AND "THE WHIRL"

It is not easy to get a tryout for a professional team. Young players frequently believe that if they could only be seen by the right coach—at the right moment—they could get their break. Twelve-year-old Johan Cruyff's break came because his mother was a cleaning woman in the team office. She knew her son was a good player, and she convinced the Ajax club coaching staff to give the boy a chance.

The Dutch youngster got his chance, and he wowed the coaches of Ajax, who put him on their youth development team. He moved quickly through the ranks, working as hard on his own as he did in practices, especially on dribbling and ball control. At age seventeen Cruyff was put in the starting lineup of the first team and never looked back.

In the 1970s Ajax was known for a type of soccer nicknamed the whirl, and Cruyff came to symbolize it more than any other player. A team using "the whirl" had more flexibility on the field because every player could play every position. Defenses would understandably become frustrated; just when they thought they had covered Ajax's forwards, a defender would bring the ball up and shoot while the forward would fall back to cover on defense! Cruyff brought that style of play to a new level, dancing from defensive midfield, to wing, and then to center midfield; few opponents could keep track of him.

After playing for Ajax and the Holland national team for years, Cruyff was lured to a professional team in Barcelona, Spain, where he achieved a great deal of success as a player and later as a coach.

the 1966 World Cup (Great Britain had relented and rejoined FIFA in 1950) the national team's coach was asked about England's chances of winning. He pointed across the field to where Moore was practicing a move with the ball.

"We're going to win," said the coach. "And that man's the reason why. He can already see in his mind's eye a picture of himself holding up the World Cup, and he's calculated down to the last detail just what that will mean to him."[50]

Moore did not disappoint his coach or his fans. In what soccer experts say was the tournament of his career, Moore played his position perfectly. After England's 4-2 win over West Germany in the finals, Moore was voted Player of Players for the World Cup tournament. Pelé, long an admirer of Moore's style and leadership abilities, called him "the finest defender in the world."[51]

Ronaldo

But not all soccer stars have contributed to the game in the same way. Ronaldo, a soccer sensation from Brazil, is a case in point. A very talented player, Ronaldo has captured not only the hearts of soccer fans but also of the advertising world.

Born Ronaldo Luis Nazano de Lima in 1976, he adopted his single-name identity in the tradition of other Brazilian soccer players, most notably Pelé. He was born in a very poor section of Rio de Janeiro, Brazil. Most of his early soccer was played either on the beach or along grassy strips near busy roads.

There were no leagues for children in these poor areas; even so, Ronaldo's skill was apparent to older players who observed him. By the time Ronaldo was sixteen, he had been given a tryout with a pro

Ronaldo's exciting style of play led to many requests for endorsements.

team—and he made it. The following year he was the only seventeen-year-old on Brazil's 1994 World Cup team.

Because of their very early successes on Brazilian teams, Ronaldo and Pelé have often been compared to each other. They are similar in some ways; they both have given defenders fits because of their excellent ball handling. Their quickness and hard shots on goal invite comparison also.

A Pre-Endorsement World

But they are more different than they are the same. Ronaldo is a strongly built young man, six feet tall and 175 pounds, with a shaved head. On the field he relies less on cunning and finesse than he does on speed and power. And unlike Pelé, who played with Brazil his whole professional career until coming to the United States, Ronaldo joined an Italian team, Inter Milan, in which he made $14 million just to sign his first year's contract.

Because of his skill and his huge salary (he is the most highly paid player in all of soccer), Ronaldo is one of the most recognized athletes in the world. He was voted World Player of the Year in 1996 and again in 1997, and because he has shown such promise, businesses are flocking to him for endorsements.

Nike offered him his own line of soccer shoes, the Ronaldo, paying him $15 mil-

lion for the right to use his name. He does commercials for beer, milk, and tires. And though his performance at the 1998 World Cup was poor, he is still in demand.

"He has charisma, he has class," explains one soccer coach. "He drives around in his silver Ferrari and lives in the swankest home in Milan. Everyone wants to be Ronaldo. In Brazil, as in Italy, he's a soccer god." [52]

Good for the Game?

Some soccer purists feel that such advertising and endorsements cheapen the game. They worry that the huge salaries and bonuses are being handed out because of a handsome face, not on the basis of value to a team.

As one soccer enthusiast explains,

I hate it in a way. Like you hate to see the multimillion-dollar salaries in any sport—it sort of takes away from the game, I think. I think about Pelé, and the little bit of money, comparatively speaking, that he got for being so loyal all those years to Brazil.

The greatest player in the history of the game, no one will ever be his equal, I'm convinced. But he got nothing like Ronaldo's getting. But Pelé's world was a pre-endorsement world. There were no fat signing bonuses, no big deals for a shoe or a soft drink with his name on it. [53]

TAKING HER ROLE SERIOUSLY—BRIANA SCURRY

Though she doesn't run up and down the field for ninety minutes like her teammates, Briana Scurry, the goalkeeper for the U.S. women's team, works just as hard. Making between twenty and thirty gutsy saves per game in international matches has put her in the media limelight, and in *Women's Soccer: The Game and the World Cup,* edited by Jim Trecker and Charles Miers, it is clear that she takes that role seriously.

Briana also thinks about her career long term—about how she influences the young people who see her play. Realizing that being a professional athlete includes off-the-field responsibilities, she is eager to do all she can to positively influence kids' lives.

"I definitely see myself as a role model for African-American kids, all kids. . . . It's hard for little African-American girls, in particular, because they see Michael Jordan, they see the Mailman [Karl Malone], they see Deion Sanders, and they're all men. And they're so far out there that they can't reach them. They're like gods, almost. When they see me out here . . . they see something that they can aspire to. . . .

"I grew up in a predominantly white suburb. Whichever sport I played, I was pretty much the only black kid on the team. It never bothered me because I

was well-received by my teammates. . . . I also thank my parents because they taught me to be well-adjusted, view the situation around me, and be friends with everyone regardless of color. But I am proud of my heritage, and I take very seriously my role of showing African-American youth, and people in general, that we can excel in sport—or in anything."

U.S. goalie Briana Scurry wants to be a role model for African American children.

However, the presence of such a rags-to-riches story as Ronaldo—as well as the exposure and fame he represents to a product—can help the game as well. By attracting more investors, and more publicity to soccer, he is generating more interest in the game. With more interest, there are more facilities and more leagues for young players.

"You can't doubt the effect of Ronaldo," says coach Jeremy Driver. "He's not Pelé—yet. Who knows, in time? But he's had an effect on the game, that's for sure. It's just been a different sort of way that he's been influential, that's all."[54]

Mia Hamm

Even more than Ronaldo, however, the U.S. women's national team has had a profound influence on the game, particularly after winning the World Cup for the second time in 1999. (The U.S. team won the first-ever Women's World Cup in 1991.) Not only did the U.S. victory increase national pride and a growing excitement about the game, it also showed the distance women's sports have come in this country. As one FIFA official says, "No other group of individuals has made a longer or a more lasting impact on the landscape of women's sports in the United States."[55]

Although the team is loaded with talent, the most prominent figure is Mia Hamm, who, at twenty-seven years old, has scored more goals in international play than any other player—male or female. She is considered the linchpin of the U.S. team's offense; she has speed, dribbling skills, and a wicked shot. Few would disagree that she is the greatest female soccer player on the planet.

Anson Dorrance, the coach of the U.S. team in the mid-1980s, recalls seeing Hamm for the first time. He had been told about this fourteen-year-old who seemed to play as though she were years older, but he was not prepared for what he encountered when he saw her play against college-age athletes. The ball was kicked off, he remembers, and "this little girl took off like she was shot out of a cannon. I thought, 'Oh, my God.' I couldn't believe the athleticism."[56]

She was fifteen when she was selected for the U.S. national team—the youngest player ever to play for a U.S. team. And rather than be intimidated by her elders, she has made it a point to learn everything she can from them. Her teammates admit that she pushes herself harder than any coach ever could.

One-on-One with Michael Jordan

Like Ronaldo, Mia Hamm has attained status as an advertising icon. She has done commercials for shampoo, and Nike has given her her own signature brand of soccer shoes. She's even become the official spokesperson for Soccer Barbie, who announces, "I can kick and throw like Mia

Hamm." Hamm's favorite, she says, is a commercial in which she goes one-on-one with Michael Jordan. Those who know her say that she and Jordan have a great deal in common besides their commercial appeal. "She has that Michael Jordan impact," says

Mia Hamm has scored more goals than any other player in international play.

one coach. "She gets the ball and everyone holds their breath. You might get to see something you've never seen before!"[57]

Hamm's contribution to the game of soccer has been more than skill and marketing, however. Together with her teammates, she has made an effort to be accessible to fans—especially young girls who emulate her. She understands, she says, the responsibility of being a role model in a relatively new sport for women. When she appears to sign autographs or is met by adoring fans after a game, she stays until every book has been signed and every fan has been greeted.

"We're going to sign for as long as it takes," she says, speaking for her team. "Every time we step on the field we know the responsibility we have. We take it very seriously."[58]

Soccer's Future

EXCITING PLAYERS HAVE increased soccer's popularity around the world. Attendance in matches in Europe, South America, and the United States is at an all-time high. However, there have been disturbing trends in soccer that have grown in recent years. If the game's future is to be a positive one, these problems need to be addressed—and soon.

Inherently Violent?

One of the most important issues is that of violence. Since its early days as a mob sport in England, soccer has had a reputation as a violent, bloody sport—one in which broken bones and black eyes were the price one paid to play. The Football Association's rules tried to curtail the in-juries by creating penalties, and that seemed to work—to an extent.

But the game grew; soon there were important matches and tournaments driving the stakes higher and higher. Because of the importance of winning—whether it be a national championship, a club match, or a world title—teams began singling out the best players on the opposing team and doing things to take them out of the game. The fouls they would commit were not tactical fouls, as one might see in the last seconds of a basketball game. Rather, these soccer fouls were intended to disable a player to the extent that he would be unable to play.

Pelé complained bitterly about it during the 1966 World Cup. He said he felt like a marked man on the field as Bulgarian opponents—and later Portuguese defenders—would do everything they could to injure him, Pelé's complaints about the cheap, obvious fouling fell on deaf ears with the referees in charge.

It was not an isolated incident against Pelé, either. Other teams noticed the increase of fouling, especially the ugliest type of fouls, called "away-from-the-ball" fouls. While the attention of the referees (and almost everyone else) was on the player with the ball, it became increasingly common for players to commit fouls against their rivals who were away from the ball.

Red Card!

By the time the next World Cup took place, soccer had a new rule. Referees now carried a yellow card and a red card. If a player was guilty of a cheap foul, the referee would flash the yellow card as a warning. If the roughness continued, a red card would be flashed, signaling that the guilty player would be ejected from the game. To make the consequences more severe, a player ejected from a game could not be replaced by a substitute; the guilty team would be forced to play one player short for the duration of the game.

This card system seemed to cut down on the fouling. Players knew

that a moment of losing their temper could result in their team being short a player and thus very vulnerable to being scored on. But while this was reassuring to many players, a great deal of violence still touched the game, particularly off the field. Violence among soccer spectators is inarguably the number one concern in soccer today.

The card system was implemented to discourage players from committing flagrant fouls.

70

Nothing New

Since people began playing soccer, the game has evoked strong, passionate emotions from fans. Everyone seems to have a favorite team within his or her nation's professional leagues, not to mention a passion for the national team when the World Cup rolls around every four years. But there is a definite line between wanting one's team to win and wishing one's opponents ill—and that line gets crossed all too frequently.

Fan violence is not at all a new phenomenon. In fact, at the very first World Cup, held in Uruguay in 1930, there was a great fear of what might happen in the championship game between Uruguay and Argentina. Because the two nations are neighbors in South America, there was an even greater sense of competition. Expecting the worst, Uruguayan police officers conducted weapons searches of all Argentine fans coming into the stadium. Interestingly, it was difficult to find referees willing to officiate at the final; only after promising police protection and life insurance.

Following Uruguay's victory in the final game, there was understandable jubilation on the part of Uruguayan fans. "Motor horns blared in triumph," writes one historian, "ships blew their sirens in the port, flags and banners flew, [and] the next day was proclaimed a national holiday."[59] The Uruguayan president, choked with emotion over his country's world-class show-

ing, declared a national holiday. Bars and taverns throughout the country stayed open all night, serving free wine and beer.

Across the river in Argentina, things were decidedly ugly. The Uruguayan embassy was stoned by a mob of thousands, and Argentine police officers dispersed it by opening fire. Two days later, formal relations were broken off between the two countries.

"A Flag that Rolls"

Unfortunately, the violence of 1930 has been repeated over and over in every decade since. Some experts say the reason is often the intense nationalism that fans feel when their team plays another country. Many of the political or economic disagreements between the countries become baggage that fans bring with them to the stadium. Because of the tight bond between soccer and homeland, writer Eduardo Galeano has gone so far as to call a soccer ball "a flag that rolls."[60]

In many instances, the tie between soccer team and national politics has had disastrous consequences. Consider, for example, the case of the famous Ukrainian team of 1942. During the German occupation of Russia, it was forced to play against a Nazi squad for the amusement of the local German troops. The Ukrainians, known as the Dynamo Kiev team, made the fatal mistake of beating their political captors: "For the Nazis, too, soccer was a matter of state. . . . Having been warned, 'If you win, you die,' [the Ukrainians] started out resigned to losing, trembling with fear and hunger, but in the end, they could not resist the temptation of dignity. When the game was over, all eleven were shot with their shirts on at the edge of a cliff."[61]

Not Heroic

But while the Ukrainian team's defeat of the Nazi squad was heroic, the zealous nationalism demonstrated at soccer games by fans is not. There are thousands of spectators—especially in Europe—who attend games more interested in stirring up trouble than in watching the players.

"It isn't just a matter of waving your own flag, or trying to sing your own anthem louder than the other fellow's," says one fan who has attended hundreds of soccer games in England and Wales. "It's hard to imagine the kind of meanness that you see at some of the matches. People come with an agenda, and the soccer's nothing important at all, not really. The game is just the setting for their little war, and it's really disruptive."[62]

In his book *The World's Game: A History of Soccer,* Bill Murray bemoans the taunting and verbal abuse that appears at soccer matches, noting that it seems to be "a universal failing that people want to taunt someone else, be it fans from the south of England mocking the unemployment of the north by

showing off their designer underwear and waving bank notes . . . or fans in Nigeria throwing bread onto the field to mock the visitors from [famine-plagued] Ethiopia."[63]

Hooligans—More than Name-Callers

There have been a huge number of incidents involving cruel, ugly words between rival groups of fans. At some European games, fans hold up signs proclaiming "Hitler was right" to insult Eastern European fans or white supremacist signs to provoke teams with black players.

And while such actions are hurtful, they seem minimal compared to the actual physical violence that was becoming all too commonplace at soccer matches in some parts of the world beginning in the 1970s. Although incidents of violence have occurred in many nations, one of the hardest-hit is England, where mobs of young male fans, known as "hooligans," attend the games with an agenda that has little to do with the sport. One soccer expert recalls how the incidents of hooliganism began in the 1970s, and have continued: "Games became the excuse for a weekly orgy of bloodletting between rival gangs of fans. Pitched battles on the terraces, field invasions, and skirmishes with the police outside the stadiums became a Saturday afternoon ritual. Excursion trains were wrecked, stores looted, innocent bystanders were often injured."[64]

In England, "hooligans" have marred the game of soccer with their combative behavior.

Nationalism certainly had nothing to do with most of the violence; after all, much of it took place at stadiums where two English professional teams were playing. Experts say the hooligans represent a very small part of soccer crowds, but they tend to be difficult to ignore. Often intoxicated and frequently shouting neo-Nazi or other racist slogans, they have been part of some of the most horrible disasters in the history of sports.

Ghastly Consequences

Hooliganism became a worldwide issue in the 1980s, as several tragedies occurred due to fan violence. One of the most pub-

licized incidents occurred on May 29, 1985, at the prestigious European Cup, in which professional teams contend to see which team is the best on that continent. The final game that day was between Italy's Juventus team and England's Liverpool team at Heysel Stadium in Brussels.

Just before the game began, a mass of drunken Liverpool fans, separated from Italian fans by a fence, stampeded the Italians. A retaining wall gave way, and thirty-nine fans were crushed to death, many of them buried in the mountains of debris under the stands. Another one hundred fans were injured. Team captains were forced to broadcast over the public address system, appealing to fans to stop the violence so that the game could be played.

FIFA has usually been reluctant to impose penalties on teams, maintaining that the violent behavior does not originate on the field or among players. It is up to the stadiums and municipalities, soccer officials have insisted, to keep order and to punish violent spectators. However, as a result of this incident, English teams were banned from participating in European Cup matches for five years.

During the 1985 European Cup, a retaining wall gave way causing injury and death to many fans.

Violence Toward Players

Recently, the out-of-control emotions among fans have affected not only other fans but also players and officials. Referees in Argentina and Peru have been threatened and shot at for making (or not making, in some cases) a controversial call.

A coach for a professional team in Russia was beaten when he declined to put a popular player on the field during an important match. The U.S. men's national team was spit on and hit with plastic bags filled with urine by angry fans in Costa Rica before an Olympic match. During the 1994 World Cup, fans burned down the home of Cameroon's goalkeeper in retaliation for his failing to stop a goal.

During that same tournament, a gifted Colombian player named Andres Escobar had the bad luck to inadvertently kick a ball into his own goal. That "own goal" as it is called, helped the United States upset the Colombian team, 2-1, and it eventually led to Colombia's elimination from the tournament. Just a few days later, back in Colombia, Escobar was gunned down. According to one account,

After eating dinner with his friends, Escobar was walking toward his car in a restaurant parking lot. Suddenly, three men began to insult him about his poor performance. One man grabbed Escobar and was heard to say, "Thanks for the own goal!" before he pulled out a pistol and started firing bullets into Escobar's face and chest. . . . With each shot the killers shouted "Goal! Goal!"[65]

Soccer enthusiasts are quick to defend their sport, saying that it is not inherently violent; after all, the game itself is nowhere near as dangerous as football or hockey. Even so, they admit that the overly passionate fans—often from the parts of society that are poorer and less educated—have tainted the sport's reputation.

A Need for Better Facilities

One improvement that is essential for soccer's well-being is a massive renovation of its stadiums around the world. Many tragedies at soccer games—including some that have been all too quickly blamed on fan behavior—have been caused by woefully inadequate facilities.

One grisly case occurred in Sheffield, England, in April 1989, just a few moments

before the start of the semifinal game of the annual Football Association Cup between Liverpool and Nottingham Forest. As a quick buildup of fans behind the turnstiles was causing a bottleneck delay, police officers opened exit gates in an area that was already filled to capacity. "It was then," writes one soccer historian, "that the slow crush built up on the spectators closest to the fence, who had no means of escape. There were no side gates, the fence was built to withstand an army, and the small exit gates were pathetically inadequate."[66] In the frantic scrambling and pushing, 95 fans were killed and 180 more were seriously injured. Many of the victims were children who were trampled to death by the frightened crowd.

In 1985, a deadly fire broke out in an outdoor stadium in Bradford, England, when someone dropped a match or cigarette

A police officer surveys the scorched remains of the outdoor stadium in Bradford.

butt under the bleachers. Rubbish under the old stands, which had been accumulating for decades, caught fire quickly, without easy exits, fans were either burned to death or were asphyxiated.

In 1992 fifteen fans were killed and thirteen hundred more were injured when a temporary stand collapsed during a soccer game.

"This kind of thing is inexcusable," notes one expert. "Many of the stadiums that teams are playing in haven't been upgraded for centuries. Just to squeeze in a few hundred more fans, we're putting people's lives in jeopardy. FIFA, as well as more local soccer authorities, needs to take a good look at soccer facilities—especially those in Europe and South America."[67]

Time Out for a Commercial Message?

While changes in the way soccer officials deal with facilities and fan behavior are certainly critical, there are a number of other less-critical issues that also affect the game and how it is played. One worry is the effect that television (especially American networks) will have on the future of soccer.

As fans in the United States become more soccer-savvy, television networks will almost certainly respond by televising more matches, both in the United States and around the world. Because of the billions of dollars that television revenue can pump into a sport, some soccer purists are concerned about what sorts of changes television will demand for its investment.

As one fan admits,

So far, things have been okay. The Olympic soccer coverage, the World Cup coverage. I wondered how the networks would get around the forty-five-minute, uninterrupted halves without commercials. But they did it, just overloading us during halftime, I guess. I just hope as coverage expands, we don't start getting all the time outs they have in football or basketball—that would really take away the simplicity of the game.[68]

Defensive Soccer

However, some fans would charge that the simplicity of the game is already eroding, even without interference from television. The creativity and spontaneity of soccer is on the wane, they say, because the sport has become too big. Money—more than $350 billion in 1996—is being generated by the sport, and it is having a negative influence.

Soccer expert Paul Gardner maintains that the money has been forcing teams to play more conservatively since the trend began in the 1980s. "Millions of dollars could now be at stake on a single result," he writes. "At the top, soccer was no longer a game to be played, it was a business venture to be calculated, to be financed—and to be organized."[69]

TOO MUCH COACHING

In his book *The Simplest Game: The Intelligent Fan's Guide to the World of Soccer,* Paul Gardner explains one of his biggest gripes about the "evolution" of modern soccer: the increased need for coaches. Too bad, he says, for soccer coaches were unheard of when the game began.

As the coach became more important, the discipline of coaching started to dress itself up in academic garb. Suddenly, there was the coaching industry. Coaching courses, licenses, and diplomas proliferated all over the world. Coaching seminars, coaching symposia, coaching workshops, and coaching clinics were all the rage. Learned treatises and books on coaching were published at an alarming rate. A pseudo-scientific coaching jargon spread across the sport. What J. C. Thring [the Englishman who first wrote down the rules] had called *The Simplest Game* in 1862 was in danger of becoming *The Most Complicated Sport.*

This sport, which had once been improvised by the players on the field, now seemed to be more about charts and diagrams and X's and O's than about people. There was not much room anymore for the freelance, inventive type of player. The coach had his plans and his tactics, and the players had to fit in, had to play their roles, and not wander off into flights of creative fantasy.

The artists were a problem for the coaches, who recognized their brilliance but didn't know what to do with them, didn't trust them to do what they were told. The coaches were right, of course. The artists couldn't be trusted to play according to instructions. The essence of their game was the sudden burst of unpredictable skill, the genius of the unexpected.

A large part of that organization meant making the game more defensive. The priority was no longer to score but to do the easier thing: to keep the other side from scoring. Dribblers and ball artists were few; with so much defense, they were unable to produce the goals they once had.

Goals were scored, certainly, but more often they were the result of plays outlined by coaches—a fact that confused many players used to a freewheeling type of soccer. As one forward complained about his coach, "The way he talks about

football [soccer] sometimes, I think it must be easier to split the atom than score a goal."[70]

Tiebreakers

Perhaps to inject some excitement into the games, which were more and more often ending in scoreless ties, FIFA introduced the shootout tiebreaker. Simply put, this was a shooting contest in which five players from each team kicked penalty kicks one-on-one against the opposing goalkeeper. The team that had the most goals after each of the five players had kicked was declared the winner. (In case the

score was still tied after five shots, each remaining player would take a kick until the tie was broken.)

While the shootout accomplishes its mission of ending a tie game, many critics believe that it does so artificially—in a way that has very little to do with real soccer. Fumes one expert,

> The penalty kick tiebreaker is a gimmick tacked on to the end of a game that has absolutely nothing to do with what has gone before, and that is very likely to reward defensively oriented teams. If a team feels that it cannot beat its opponents by playing soccer during the regular game, the alternative is to play defensively for 120 minutes, get the tie, then trust to the 50-50 tiebreaker.[71]

Many professional coaches say they would rather have the game end as a tie than use the shootout. Others have suggested finding a tiebreaker that would actually encourage offensive play. For example, Paul Gardner has suggested that in case of a tie, referees should award the win to the team who had the most corner kicks during the game. (A corner kick is awarded to an attacking team if a defensive player touches the ball before it goes over the end line; it is a great scoring opportunity to be given a corner kick.) As Gardner explains, "To get corner kicks, a team had to attack, it had to get down the other end of the field. If it

A REACTION TO PENALTY KICK SHOOTOUTS

In his book *Soccer in Sun and Shadow*, Eduardo Galeano offers a brief essay in which he gives his reaction to FIFA's idea of breaking tie games with a shootout. The essay is aptly titled "Indigestion."

> In 1989 in Buenos Aires, a match between Argentinos Juniors and Racing ended in a draw. The rules called for a penalty kick shootout.

> The crowd was on its feet, biting its nails, for the first shots at twelve paces. The fans cheered a goal by Racing. Then came a goal by Argentinos Juniors and the fans from the other side cheered. There was an ovation when the Racing keeper leapt against one post and sent the ball awry. Another ovation praised the Argentinos keeper who did not allow himself to be seduced by the expression on the striker's face, and waited for the ball in the center of the goal.

> When the tenth penalty was kicked, there was another round of applause. A few fans left the stadium after the twentieth goal. When the thirtieth penalty came around, the few who remained responded with yawns. Kicks came and went and the match remained tied.

> After forty-four penalty kicks, the game ended. It was a world record for penalties. In the stadium no one was left to celebrate, and no one even knew which side won.

Some coaches have suggested that tiebreakers be awarded to teams with the most corner kicks at the end of a game.

played defensively, camped in its own half, it would inevitably give up corners and not gain any."[72] However, FIFA has yet to abandon its shootout strategy.

"The Passion Most Widely Shared"

No matter how irritated its fans become at the game, however, soccer seems to be able to win them back. Like no other game, it seems to cross political, economic, and racial boundaries; the language of soccer is universal.

Soccer has evolved from its roots in long-ago civilizations. From being a mob free-for-all that kings and queens tried to ban and the game of the close-cropped playing fields of English boarding schools, the sport was transported to the poorest slums of Brazilian cities and became a World Cup event watched by over 2 billion people around the globe. It is, today, what one writer calls "the passion most widely shared."[73]

As much as coaches and other technical people try to make the game a science, as much as some players might try to turn it into a rough or plodding contest, a player or team comes along to show that it is art nonetheless. Soccer has a way, says writer Eduardo Galeano, of surviving "in spite of all the spites."[74]

Awards and Statistics

The World Cup

The Federation Internationale de Football Association (FIFA) began the World Cup championship tournament in 1930 with a 13-team field in Uruguay. Sixty-four years later, 138 countries competed in qualifying rounds to fill 24 berths in the 1994 World Cup finals. FIFA increased the World Cup 1998 tournament field from 24 to 32 teams, including automatic berths for defending champion Brazil and host France. The other 30 slots were allotted by region: Europe (14) Africa (5), South America (4) CONCACAF (3), Asia (3), and the one remaining position to the winner of a playoff between the fourth place team in Asia and the champion of Oceania.

The United States hosted the World Cup for the first time in 1994 and American crowds shattered tournament attendance records. . . . Tournaments have now been played three times in North America (Mexico 2 and U.S.), four times in South America (Argentina, Chile, Brazil and Uruguay) and nine times in Europe (France 2, Italy 2, England, Spain, Sweden, Switzerland and West Germany).

Brazil retired the first World Cup (called the Jules Rimet Trophy after FIFA's first president) in 1970 after winning it for the third time. The new trophy, first presented in 1974, is known as simply the World Cup.

Multiple winners: Brazil (4); Italy and West Germany (3); Argentina and Uruguay (2).

Year	Champion	Manager	Score	Runner-up	Host Country	Third Place
2002	at Japan/South Korea					
1998	France	Aimé Jacquet	3-0	Brazil	France	Croatia 2, Holland 1
1994	Brazil	Carlos Parreira	0-0	Italy	USA	Sweden 4, Bulgaria 0
1990	W. Germany	Franz Beckenbauer	1-0	Argentina	Italy	Italy 2, England 1
1986	Argentina	Carlos Bilardo	3-2	W. Germany	Mexico	France 4, Belgium 2
1982	Italy	Enzo Bearzot	3-1	W. Germany	Spain	Poland 3, France 2
1978	Argentina	Cesar Menotti	3-1	Holland	Argentina	Brazil 2, Italy 1
1974	W. Germany	Helmut Schoen	2-1	Holland	W. Germany	Poland 1, Brazil 0
1970	Brazil	Mario Zagalo	4-1	Italy	Mexico	W. Ger. 1, Uruguay 0
1966	England	Alf Ramsey	4-2	W. Germany	England	Portugal 2, USSR 1
1962	Brazil	Aimoré Moreira	3-1	Czechoslovakia	Chile	Chile 1, Yugoslavia 0
1958	Brazil	Vicente Feola	5-2	Sweden	Sweden	France 6, W. Ger. 3
1954	W. Germany	Sepp Herberger	3-2	Hungary	Switzerland	Austria 3, Uruguay 1
1950	Uruguay	Juan Lopez	2-1	Brazil	Brazil	No game
1942–46	Not held					
1938	Italy	Vittório Pozzo	4-2	Hungary	France	Brazil 4, Sweden 2
1934	Italy	Vittório Pozzo	2-1	Czechoslovakia	Italy	Germany 3, Austria 2
1930	Uruguay	Alberto Suppici	4-2	Argentina	Uruguay	No game

All-Time World Cup Leaders

World Cup scoring leaders throughout 1998. Years listed are years played in World Cup.

	No.
Gerd Müller, West Germany (1970, 74)	14
Just Fontaine, France (1958)	13
Pelé, Brazil (1958, 62, 66, 70)	12
Sandor Kocsis, Hungary (1954)	11
Juergen Klinsmann, Germany (1990, 94, 98)	11
Helmut Rahn, West Germany (1954, 58)	10
Teofilo Cubillas, Peru (1970, 78)	10
Gregorz Lato, Poland (1974, 78, 82)	10
Gary Lineker, England (1986, 90)	10

All-Time World Cup Ranking Table

Since the first World Cup in 1930, Brazil is the only country to play in all 16 final tournaments. The FIFA all-time table below ranks all nations that have ever qualified for a World Cup final tournament by points earned through 1998. Victories, which earned two points from 1930–1990, were awarded three points starting in 1994. Note that Germany's appearances include 10 made by West Germany from 1954–1990. Participants in the 1998 World Cup final are in **bold** type.

		App	Gm	W	L	T	Pts	GF	GA
1	**Brazil**	16	80	53	13	14	**120**	173	78
2	**Germany**	14	78	45	16	17	**107**	162	103
3	**Italy**	14	66	38	12	16	**92**	105	62
4	**Argentina**	12	57	29	18	10	**68**	100	69
5	**England**	10	45	20	12	13	**53**	62	42
6	**France**	10	41	21	14	6	**48**	86	58
7	**Spain**	10	40	16	14	10	**42**	61	48
8	**Yugoslavia**	9	37	16	13	8	**40**	60	46
9	Uruguay	9	37	15	14	8	**38**	61	52
	Russia	8	34	16	12	6	**38**	60	40
11	Sweden	9	38	14	15	9	**37**	66	60
	Netherlands	7	31	14	9	9	**37**	56	36
13	Hungary	9	32	15	14	3	**33**	87	57
14	Poland	5	25	13	7	5	**31**	39	29
15	**Austria**	7	29	12	13	4	**28**	43	47
16	Czech Republic	8	30	11	14	5	**27**	44	45
17	**Mexico**	11	37	8	19	10	**26**	39	75
18	**Belgium**	10	32	9	16	7	**25**	40	56
19	**Romania**	7	21	8	8	5	**21**	30	32
20	**Chile**	7	25	7	12	6	**20**	31	40
21	**Scotland**	8	23	4	12	7	**15**	25	41
	Switzerland	7	22	6	13	3	**15**	33	51
23	**Bulgaria**	7	26	3	15	8	**14**	22	53
	Paraguay	5	15	4	6	5	**14**	19	27
25	**Cameroon**	4	14	3	5	6	**12**	13	26
	Portugal	2	9	6	3	0	**12**	19	12
27	Peru	4	15	4	8	3	**11**	19	31
	N. Ireland	3	13	3	5	5	**11**	13	23
	Denmark	2	9	5	3	1	**11**	19	13
30	**Croatia**	1	7	5	2	0	**10**	11	5
31	**USA**	6	17	4	12	1	**9**	18	38
32	**Morocco**	4	13	2	7	4	**8**	12	18
	Colombia	4	13	3	8	2	**8**	14	23
	Nigeria	2	8	4	4	0	**8**	13	13
35	Ireland	2	9	1	3	5	**7**	4	7
	Norway	2	8	2	3	3	**7**	7	8
37	East Germany	1	6	2	2	2	**6**	5	5
38	**Saudi Arabia**	2	7	2	4	1	**5**	7	13
	Algeria	2	6	2	3	1	**5**	6	10
	Wales	1	5	1	1	3	**5**	4	4
41	**South Korea**	5	14	0	10	4	**4**	11	43
	Tunisia	2	6	1	3	2	**4**	4	6
	Costa Rica	1	4	2	2	0	**4**	4	6
44	**Iran**	2	6	1	4	1	**3**	4	12
	North Korea	1	4	1	2	1	**3**	5	9
	Cuba	1	3	1	1	1	**3**	5	12
	Jamaica	1	3	1	2	0	**3**	3	9
48	Egypt	2	4	0	2	2	**2**	3	6
	Honduras	1	3	0	1	2	**2**	2	3
	Israel	1	3	0	1	2	**2**	1	3
	Turkey	1	3	1	2	0	**2**	10	11
	South Africa	1	3	0	1	2	**2**	3	6
53	Bolivia	3	6	0	5	1	**1**	1	20
	Australia	1	3	0	2	1	**1**	0	5
	Kuwait	1	3	0	2	1	**1**	2	6
56	El Salvador	2	6	0	6	0	**0**	1	22
	Canada	1	3	0	3	0	**0**	0	5
	East Indies	1	1	0	1	0	**0**	0	6
	Greece	1	3	0	3	0	**0**	0	10
	Haiti	1	3	0	3	0	**0**	2	14
	Iraq	1	3	0	3	0	**0**	1	4
	Japan	1	3	0	3	0	**0**	1	4
	New Zealand	1	3	0	3	0	**0**	2	12
	UAE	1	3	0	3	0	**0**	2	11
	Zaire	1	3	0	3	0	**0**	0	14

The United States in the World Cup

While the United States has fielded a national team every year of the World Cup, only five of those teams have been able to make it past the preliminary competition and qualify for the final World Cup tournament. The 1994 national team automatically qualified because the United States served as host of the event for the first time. The United States played in three of the first four World Cups (1930, 1934, and 1950) and each of the last three (1990, 1994 and 1998). The Americans have a record of 4-12-1 in 17 World Cup matches, with two victories in 1930, a 1-0 upset of England in 1950, and a 2-1 shocker over Colombia in 1994.

1998

1st Round Matches

Germany 2	United States 0
Iran 2	United States 1
Yugoslavia 1	United States 0

U.S. Scoring—Brian McBride.

1994

1st Round Matches

United States 1	Switzerland 1
United States 2	Colombia 1
Romania 1	United States 0

Round of 16

Brazil 1	United States 0

Overall U.S. Scoring—Eric Wynalda, Ernie Stewart and own goal (Colombia defender Andres Escobar).

1990

1st Round Matches

Czechoslovakia 5	United States 1
Italy 1	United States 0
Austria 2	United States 1

U.S. Scoring—Paul Caligiuri and Bruce Murray.

1950

1st Round Matches

Spain 3	United States 1
United States 1	England 0
Chili 5	United States 2

U.S. Scoring—Joe Gaetjens, Joa Maca, John Souza and Frank Wallace.

1934

1st Round Match

Italy 7	Unites States 1

U.S. Scoring—Buff Donelli (who later became a noted college and NFL football coach).

1930

1st Round Matches

United States 3	Belgium 0
United States 3	Paraguay 0

Semifinals

Argentina 6	United States 1

U.S. Scoring—Bert Patenaude (3), Bart McGhee (2), James Brown and Thomas Florie.

FIFA Top Fifty World Rankings

FIFA announced a new monthly world ranking system on August 13, 1993 designed to "provide a constant international comparison of national team performances." The rankings are based on a mathematical formula that weighs strength of schedule, importance of matches and goals scored for and against. Games considered include World Cup qualifying and final rounds, Continental championship qualifying and final rounds, and friendly matches.

The formula was altered slightly in January 1999. Now the rankings annually take into account a team's seven best matches of the last eight years. Thereby favoring some teams that have been consistent over a long period of time but that may have stumbled just recently. At the end of the year, FIFA designates a Team of the Year. Teams of the Year so far have been Germany (1993) and Brazil (1994–1998).

1999 (as of September 15)

		Points	1998 Rank
1	Brazil	838	1
2	Czech Republic	772	8
3	France	766	2
4	Spain	757	15
5	Germany	735	3
6	Croatia	727	4
7	Argentina	717	5
8	Italy	714	7

		Points	1998 Rank
9	Norway	712	14
10	Mexico	709	10
	Romania	709	12
12	England	683	9
13	Portugal	671	36
14	Netherlands	668	11
15	Sweden	667	18
16	Denmark	661	19
17	Yugoslavia	656	6
18	Paraguay	647	25
19	Russia	642	40
20	**USA**	621	23
21	Morocco	620	13
	Slovakia	620	32
23	Colombia	619	34
24	Chile	618	16
	Israel	618	43
26	Austria	615	22
	Ukraine	615	47
28	Scotland	606	38
29	Poland	595	31
30	Tunisia	593	21
31	South Africa	591	26
32	Belgium	589	35
33	Zambia	582	29
34	Rep. of Ireland	576	56
35	Turkey	577	57
36	Bulgaria	570	49
37	Greece	568	53
38	Egypt	565	28
	Saudi Arabia	565	30
40	South Korea	559	17
41	Uruguay	557	76
42	Trinidad and Tobago	554	51
43	Hungary	547	46
	Jamaica	547	33
45	Peru	546	72
46	Lithuania	543	54
	Ghana	543	48
48	Ivory Coast	541	44
49	Iceland	536	64
50	Iran	534	27

World Team of the 20th Century

The team, comprised of the century's best players, was voted on by a panel that included 250 interna-tional soccer journalists and released on June 10, 1998 in conjunction with the opening of the 1998 World Cup. The panel first selected the European and South American Teams of the Century and then chose the World Team from those two lists.

> **Position key**
> GK: Goalkeeper
> MF: Midfielder
> D: Defender
> F: Fullback

World Team

Pos	
GK	Lev Yashin, Soviet Union
D	Carlos Alberto, Brazil
D	Franz Beckenbauer, West Germany
D	Bobby Moore, England
D	Nilton Santos, Brazil
MF	Johan Cruyff, Netherlands
MF	Alfredo Di Stefano, Argentina
MF	Michel Platini, France
F	Pelé, Brazil
F	Garrincha, Brazil
F	Diego Maradona, Argentina

The Olympic Games

Held every four years since 1896, except during World War I (1916) and World War II (1940–1944). Soccer was not a medal sport in 1896 at Athens or in 1932 at Los Angeles. By agreement between FIFA and the IOC, Olympic soccer com-petition is currently limited to players 23-years old and under.

Multiple winners: England and Hungary (3); Soviet Union and Uruguay (2).

Men

Year	
1996	**Nigeria**, Argentina, Brazil
1992	**Spain,** Poland, Ghana
1988	**Soviet Union**, Brazil, West Germany
1984	**France**, Brazil, Yugoslavia
1980	**Czechoslovakia**, East Germany, Soviet Union
1976	**East Germany**, Poland, Soviet Union
1972	**Poland**, Hungary, East Germany
1968	**Hungary**, Bulgaria, Japan

Year
1964 **Hungary**, Czechoslovakia, East Germany
1960 **Yugoslavia**, Denmark, Hungary
1956 **Soviet Union**, Yugoslavia, Bulgaria
1952 **Hungary**, Yugoslavia, Sweden
1948 **Sweden**, Yugoslavia, Denmark
1936 **Italy**, Austria, Norway
1928 **Uruguay**, Argentina, Italy
1924 **Uruguay**, Switzerland, Sweden
1920 **Belgium**, Spain, Holland
1912 **England**, Denmark, Holland
1908 **England**, Denmark, Holland
1906 **Denmark**, Smyrna (Int'l entry), Greece

Year
1904 **Canada**, USA I, USA II
1900 **England**, France, Belgium

Women's World Cup

First held in 1991. Officially, the FIFA Women's World Championship.
   Multiple Winners: United States (2).

Year
1999 United States
1995 Norway
1991 United States

Notes

Introduction: The Beautiful Game"

1. Anna Kriess interview by author, October 12, 1999.
2. Gerry Dolan, telephone interview by author, August 12, 1999.
3. Dolan interview.
4 Rich L. Smith, interview by author, Minneapolis, Minnesota, December 6, 1999.

Chapter 1: From Hazy Beginnings

5. Eduardo Galeano, *Soccer in Sun and Shadow*, trans. Mark Fried. New York: Verso, 1998, p. 24.
6. Quoted in Paul Gardner, *The Simplest Game: The Intelligent Fan's Guide to the World of Soccer.* New York: Collier Books, 1994, p. 3.
7. Quoted in Gardner, *The Simplest Game,* p. 3.
8. Quoted in Galeano, *Soccer in Sun and Shadow*, p. 23.
9. Quoted in Gardner, *The Simplest Game,* p. 4.
10. Quoted in Gardner, *The Simplest Game,* p. 4.
11. Quoted in Gardner, *The Simplest Game,* p. 6.
12. Quoted in Gardner, *The Simplest Game,* p. 9.
13. Quoted in Gardner, *The Simplest Game,* p. 14.
14. Billy Murray, *The World's Game: A History of Soccer.* Urbana: University of Illinois Press, 1996, p. 15.

Chapter 2: Fine–Tuning the Game

15. Quoted in Gardner, *The Simplest Game,* p. 8.
16. Galeano, *Soccer in Sun and Shadow,* p. 26.
17. Murray, *The World's Game,* p. 8.
18. Galeano, *Soccer in Sun and Shadow,* pp. 4–5.
19. Gardner, *The Simplest Game,* p. 11.

Chapter 3: The Changing Face of Soccer

20. Murray, *The World's Game,* pp. 8–9.
21. Tony Mason, *Passion of the People? Football in South America.* London: Verso, 1995, p. 4.
22. Galeano, *Soccer in Sun and Shadow,* p. 28.

23. Quoted in Paul Gardner, *SoccerTalk: Life Under the Spell of the Round Ball.* Chicago: Masters, 1999, p. 16.

24. Quoted in Galeano, *Soccer in Sun and Shadow,* p. 31.

25. Quoted in Mason, *Passion of the People?* p. 14.

26. Quoted in Mason, *Passion of the People?* pp. 18–19.

27. Galeano, *Soccer in Sun and Shadow,* p. 30.

28. Gardner, *SoccerTalk,* p. 16.

29. Galeano, *Soccer in Sun and Shadow,* p. 31.

30. Murray, *The World's Game,* p. 43.

31. Quoted in Gardner, *The Simplest Game,* p. 18.

32. Galeano, *Soccer in Sun and Shadow,* p. 45.

33. Quoted in Galeano, *Soccer in Sun and Shadow,* p. 45.

34. Quoted in Brian Glanville, *History of the Soccer World Cup.* New York: Collier, 1973, p. 8.

35. Gardner, *The Simplest Game,* p. 21.

36. Galeano, *Soccer in Sun and Shadow,* p. 56.

37. Gardner, *The Simplest Game,* p. 23.

Chapter 4: The Game's Finest

38. Henry Kissinger, "The Phenomenon: Pelé," *Time,* June 14, 1999, p. 110.

39. Quoted in Kissinger, "The Phenomenon," p. 111.

40. Ian Thomsen, "A Great Revelation Was Afoot: Pelé Makes His World Cup Debut," *Sports Illustrated,* November 29, 1999, p. 37.

41. Hank Hersch, "Pelé: Forty for the Ages," *Sports Illustrated,* September 19, 1994, p. 123.

42. Quoted in Mason, *Passion of the People?* p. 88.

43. Gardner, *SoccerTalk,* p. 101.

44. Quoted in Hersch, "Pelé," p. 122.

45. Quoted in Hersch, "Pelé," p. 123.

46. Gardner, *SoccerTalk,* p. 97.

47. Galeano, *Soccer in Sun and Shadow,* p. 120.

48. Quoted in Martin Tyler, *Soccer: The World Game.* New York: St. Martin's, 1978, p. 148.

49. Quoted in Gardner, *SoccerTalk,* p. 152.

50. Quoted in Tyler, *Soccer,* p. 149.

51. Quoted in Tyler, *Soccer,* p. 151.

52. Paul Meadows, telephone interview by author, February 2, 2000.

53. Gerry Reynolds, telephone interview by author, February 18, 2000.

54. Jeremy Driver, interview by author, Minneapolis, Minnesota, February 10, 2000.

55. Quoted in Jim Trecker and Charles Miers, eds., *Women's Soccer: The Game and the World Cup.* New York: Universe, 1999, p. 5.

56. Quoted in Mark Starr, "Keeping Her Own Score: The World Cup Will Show Everyone How Good Mia Hamm Is.

Why Can't She See It?" *Newsweek,* June 21, 1999, p. 60.

57. Quoted in Starr, "Keeping Her Own Score," p. 62.

58. Quoted in Trecker and Miers, *Women's Soccer,* pp. 62–65.

Chapter 5: Soccer's Future

59. Glanville, *History of the Soccer World Cup,* p. 16.

60. Galeano, *Soccer in Sun and Shadow,* p. 34.

61. Galeano, *Soccer in Sun and Shadow,* p. 35.

62. Dolan, telephone interview by author, January 15, 2000.

63. Murray, *The World's Game,* p. 171.

64. Gardner, *The Simplest Game,* p. 202.

65. Timothy Ross, Jonathan Freedlam, and Noll Scott, "Death of a 'Caballero,'" *World Press Review*, September 1994, p. 29.

66. Murray, *The World's Game,* p. 106.

67. John Evert interview, January 15, 2000.

68. Derek Anderson, interview by author, February 12, 2000.

69. Gardner, *The Simplest Game,* p. 198.

70. Quoted in Gardner, *The Simplest Game,* p. 201.

71. Gardner, *The Simplest Game,* p. 206.

72. Gardner, *The Simplest Game,* p. 207.

73. Galeano, *Soccer in Sun and Shadow,* p. 208.

74. Galeano, *Soccer in Sun and Shadow,* p. 208.

For Further Reading

Norman Barrett, *The World Cup.* New York: Thomsen Learning, 1993. This easy-to-read book has excellent photographs and player profiles.

Walt Chyzowych, *The World Cup.* South Bend, IN: Icarus, 1982. Contains good game-by-game accounts of some of the best World Cup matches. It also offers an interesting, though somewhat dated, section on modern trends in soccer strategies for the World Cup.

Bill Gutman, *World Cup Action!* Mahwah, NJ: Watermill, 1994. A very readable book with excellent color photographs.

Christopher Merrill, *The Grass of Another Country: A Journey Through the World of Soccer.* New York: Henry Holt, 1993. This book has a well-written narrative, especially pertaining to segments about World Cup matches.

Mark Stewart, *Soccer: A History of the World's Most Popular Game.* New York: Franklin Watts, 1998. This readable text has appendices with team statistics.

Elio Trifari and Charles Miers, eds., *Soccer! The Game and the World Cup.* New York: Rizzoli, 1994. Contains excellent action photos as well as an interesting section on fan violence.

Websites

American Youth Soccer Association (www.soccer.org). This website provides information for fans, coaches, and parents and highlights events and games that might be of interest to soccer lovers.

Soccer America (www.socceramerica.com). This site provides news about U.S. soccer teams, game highlights, and so on. There is an interactive feature concerning MLS (Major League Soccer), World Cup, Olympics, college teams of interest, and men's and women's U.S. National Teams.

Works Consulted

Books

Bill Buford, *Among the Thugs: The Experience, and the Seduction, of Crowd Violence.* New York: W. W. Norton, 1991. Very intense reading for anyone interested in the seeds of violence in society today.

Sam Foulds and Paul Harris, *America's Soccer Heritage.* Manhattan Beach, CA: Soccer for Americans, 1979. An excellent background on early American soccer leagues and personalities.

Eduardo Galeano, *Soccer in Sun and Shadow.* Trans. Mark Fried. New York: Verso, 1998. Extremely engaging writing style, with fascinating insights into South American soccer.

Paul Gardner, *The Simplest Game: The Intelligent Fan's Guide to the World of Soccer.* New York: Collier Books, 1994. Highly readable, with good background on the game's beginnings.

———, *SoccerTalk: Life Under the Spell of the Round Ball.* Chicago: Masters, 1999. Contains helpful essays, especially those about current soccer issues.

Brian Glanville, *History of the Soccer World Cup.* New York: Collier, 1973. Provides detailed accounts of the matches and players of the World Cup.

———, *Story of the World Cup.* London: Faber and Faber, 1993. Well-documented, with helpful illustrations and statistics.

Tony Mason, *Passion of the People? Football in South America.* London: Verso, 1995. Provides excellent background on Brazilian soccer as well as a good index.

Bill Murray, *The World's Game: A History of Soccer.* Urbana: University of Illinois Press, 1996. Contains helpful appendices and a thorough index.

Keir Radnedge, ed., *The Ultimate Encyclopedia of Soccer: The Definitive Illustrated Guide to World Soccer.* Rocklin, CA: Prima, 1994. Offers excellent player profiles as well as a helpful section on early rules of the game.

Jim Trecker and Charles Miers, eds., *Women's Soccer: The Game and the World Cup.* New York: Universe, 1999.

A good background on the U.S. women's team of 1994.

Martin Tyler, *Soccer: The World Game.* New York: St. Martin's, 1978. A good section on the history of the World Cup, and good action photography.

Periodicals

Hank Hersch, "Pelé: Forty for the Ages," *Sports Illustrated*, September 19, 1994.

Henry Kissinger, "The Phenomenon: Pelé," *Time,* June 14, 1999.

Melissa Levy, "Soccer Goods Retailers Hope to Win Big with Sport's Growing Popularity," *Knight-Ridder/Tribune Business News,* May 27, 1997.

Timothy Ross, Jonathan Freedland, and Noll Scott, "Death of a 'Caballero,'" *World Press Review,* September 1994.

Mark Starr, "Keeping Her Own Score: The World Cup Will Show Everyone How Good Mia Hamm Is. Why Can't She See It?" *Newsweek,* June 21, 1999.

Ian Thomas, "A Great Revelation Was Afoot: Pelé Makes His World Cup Debut," *Sports Illustrated*, November 29, 1999.

Index

Picture Credits

Cover photo: © Hulton-Deutsch Collection/Corbis
© AFP/Corbis, 65
Archive Photos, 15
© Bettmann/Corbis, 55, 57
David Cannon/Allsport, 74
Central Press/Archive Photos, 60
© Ken Chernus/FPG International, 11
© Jim Cummins/FPG International, 29, 31, 70
© Hulton-Deutsch Collection/Corbis, 47, 73
Hulton Getty/Archive Photos, 19, 21, 22, 26, 35, 36, 39, 41, 43, 54, 59, 61
Library of Congress, 46
Simon Miles/Allsport, 75
North Wind Picture Archives, 18
Doug Pensinger/Allsport, 79
Popperfoto/Archive Photos, 48, 51, 58
© Reuters Newmedia Inc/Corbis, 10
Reuters/Fatih Saribas/Archive Photos, 63
Ezra O. Shaw/Allsport, 67
© VCG/FPG International, 13, 17, 27, 33

About the Author

Gail B. Stewart received her undergraduate degree from Gustavus Adolphus College in St. Peter, Minnesota. She did her graduate work in English, linguistics, and curriculum study at the College of St. Thomas and the University of Minnesota. She taught English and reading for more than ten years.

She has written over ninety books for young people, including a series for Lucent Books called the Other America. She has written many books on historical topics such as World War I and the Warsaw ghetto.

Stewart and her husband live in Minneapolis with their three sons, Ted, Elliot, and Flynn; two dogs; and a cat. When she is not writing she enjoys reading, walking, and watching her sons play soccer.